/

THE BULLDOG

Yesterday, Today and Tomorrow

John F. McGibbon

**HOWELL
BOOK
HOUSE**

New York

Howell Book House
A Simon & Schuster Macmillan Company
1633 Broadway
New York, NY 10019

MACMILLAN is a registered trademark of Macmillan, Inc.

Library of Congress Cataloging-in-Publication Data
McGibbon, John F.
The Bulldog: yesterday, today and tomorrow/John F. McGibbon.
p. cm.

ISBN: 0-87605-070-4

1. Bulldog. I. Title
SF429.B85M35 1995
636.7'2—dc20   95-44037 CIP

Manufactured in the United States of America
10 9 8 7 6 5 4 3 2 1

DEDICATION

To
Susan Brown McGibbon
who did not realize what she was getting into
when I sold her her first Bulldog, "McLintock's Crumpet"

Reproduction of the well-known oil painting, Portraits of Rosa and Crib, two celebrated Bulldogs, the property of a Gentleman (circa 1816).—Abraham Cooper, R.A.

Wasp, Child and Billy.—Ward after Chalon (circa 1809).

Contents

Billy, Rose and Tumbler, owned by Frank Redmond, from an 1834 engraving of the painting by Dean Wolstenholme Jr.

Jem Burns's four pets—Jack Shepherd, Duchess, Crib and Ball.

Foreword

The Bulldog has always occupied a very special place in the family of purebred dogs and those who love him best treasure that singular stature. This breed is a blending of the different and the familiar and has won a legion of friends exactly because of so many contrasting aspects of character.

Truly, the Bulldog may be thought of as a living history lesson and his development a commentary on how far we have progressed as an enlightened society. *The Bulldog: Yesterday, Today and Tomorrow* looks at the Bulldog's past in historical perspective, but more importantly, it looks at the breed and how we relate to it at the present time. This is a book for the Bulldog fan of today, for the pet owner, new or experienced, the fancier, the breeder, the dog show exhibitor, the judge and the collector of Bulldog memorabilia. All can find something of lasting value in these pages.

John F. McGibbon has been a friend of the Bulldog for many years and gives readers the benefit of his extensive hands-on experience as a successful exhibitor, breeder and Specialty judge. He came to our attention exactly because he personified the enthusiast that successfully combines the love for his chosen with the scholarship to truly understand it and to help others more thoroughly enjoy the place Bulldogs occupy in their lives. We hope you, too, will enjoy this all-new work and make it an important, enduring part of your permanent Bulldog library.

THE PUBLISHER

Am., Can. Int. Ch. JB Rare McClintock, T.T., a multiple Specialty and Best in Show winner, bred by John and Susan McGibbon and D. Williams.—Carl Lindemaier

Acknowledgments

There have been many contributors to this book, either directly or indirectly. Joe Kelley, Ray Belanger and Lillian (Knight) Davis of the San Francisco Bay Area can share the credit or the blame for getting me started in Bulldogs as a serious hobby. Some, I am sure, are judging in Bulldog heaven, the foremost of whom is Arthur Westlake, no doubt still gesticulating to the audience gathered at ringside to be certain that they too can see the faults and virtues in the dog that he is judging and understand his thinking in evaluating the Bulldogs before him.

Others are still judging and engaging in fervent discussions about every endless facet of Bulldogs. These fanciers continue to be immensely helpful to anyone whom they feel is seriously interested in this unique breed. Wally and Birdie Newbill, both past presidents of the Bulldog Club of America, are such people. I first met the Newbills over twenty years ago, and it is gratifying to know that the endeavor that has resulted in this book has had their support and approval from the beginning.

Having introduced a few "newcomers" to the Bulldog breed over the years, and having had to answer the same questions on the same subjects from different people at different times, I started compiling notes regarding the most frequently asked questions. My answers were often in conflict with the written opinions of acknowledged "experts" who, although they were documented Bulldog owners, never owned a bitch nor raised a litter of puppies. Not surprisingly, the secondhand advice gleaned from their articles could be misleading and confusing. One of the most important purposes of this book is to make a meaningful attempt to remedy this tendency, and provide as much practical information on owning and enjoying Bulldogs as is possible in one source.

Dr. Michael Butchko and Dr. Alfred Plechner, wonderful veterinarians with whom I have enjoyed a long, fruitful association as a client, have unselfishly shared their impressive knowledge and peerless veterinary expertise for the benefit of every reader.

Special thanks to my editor, Seymour Weiss, whose faith, patience, understanding and encouragement have been superb. My deepest thanks also to all those who have contributed their precious photographs for inclusion in this book. For the owners of photos that could not be included, remember what so many judges often are heard to say, "There just were not enough spaces to go around."

Libby Moses, fellow writer and Bulldog breeder, is largely responsible for getting me to write this book to begin with. My computer thanks Libby's brother Chris Moses and his cohort John Bartelink, both of Papyrus Technology, for magically retrieving, on many occasions, pieces of the manuscript that I inadvertently messed up; and to Bob Kerr for showing me that old Bulldoggers can learn new computer tricks.

JOHN FRAME McGIBBON

CHAPTER

1

The History of the Bulldog

THE BULLDOG WAS ORIGINALLY KNOWN AS THE BRITISH BULLDOG, AND WAS never at any time properly referred to as the English Bulldog. That common name is a complete misnomer. The Bulldog is without question a product of the British Isles and is, to the minds of many, the most quintessential symbol of his homeland. Although the foregoing cannot be conclusively proved, it is a generally accepted fact. The Bulldog may have been in existence since the third century, but under another name, and its first *"usefulness"* was for bullbaiting.

It is difficult to say when this old English *sport* first started. However, in *The Survey of Stamford* the following reference is made to bullbaiting's possible origin:

> William Earl Warren, Lord of this town in the reign of King John (1209), standing upon the walls of his castle at Stamford, saw two bulls fighting for a cow in the castle meadows, 'till all the butchers' dogs pursued one of the bulls, which was maddened by the noise and multitude, through the town. This sight so pleased the Earl that he gave the castle meadow where the bulls' combat

The Baited Bull Broke Loose, *an 1802 print, was originally published in color and shows a group of Bulldogs of the period trying to stop a runaway bull.*

began, for a common to the butchers of the town after the first grass was mowed, on condition that they should find a "mad bull" on a day six weeks before Christmas for continuance of that sport forever.

This may have been the origin of the "sport" of bullbaiting, which increased in popularity with the passing years. Social conditions having created the demand, the supply of dogs suited to this purpose had to be filled. These dogs were carefully bred by selection; beauty and symmetry of form were not a consideration. The appearance of the dog was without meaning—only courage, power and ferocity were the desirable results. From about the thirteenth to the eighteenth centuries, bullbaiting was as much a national sport in England as baseball is in the United States and Japan, and football (soccer) is to Europe and the rest of the world today.

There is on record the will of one George Staverton, dated May 15, 1661, by which he gave the whole rent of his house situated at Staines, near London, to buy a bull annually forever, which bull he gave to the

Bullbaiting with an Iberian twist was a popular variation on the diversion circa 1814.

town of Wokingham, in Berkshire, to be there baited, then slaughtered and equally divided, the money collected from spectators to be laid out in shoes and stockings to be distributed to the children of the poor.

In 1778, the Duke of Devonshire, then Steward of Tutbury, in Staffordshire, succeeded in abolishing bullbaiting, an annual occurrence in his dukedom since 1374. Local lore has it that the cruelties exercised at that particular district were of such a sickening character that they could not be recorded. With the passing of time, sentiments began to rise against this most barbarous of "sports," although some "gentlemen" were much in favor of its continuance. A Mr. Windham stated in the House of Commons in 1801 that "the sport kept alive the spirit of the English character." Shortly thereafter the sport declined and soon became illegal to the vast majority of the citizenry. Unfortunately, there were those that still bred the dogs and profited from the various exhibitions that pitted Bulldogs against rats, lions, club-wielding monkeys, bears and other Bulldogs.

The hideous tales of human-inspired barbarism involving the use of Bulldogs has been well documented in *The New Complete Bulldog* by Colonel Bailey C. Hanes (1990, New York, Howell Book House). This

However revolting bullbaiting may seem to us today, it did dictate form and function of the dogs that ultimately developed into the modern Bulldog. Judging from the attire of the men in this illustration, it is obvious that bullbaiting in the eighteenth and nineteenth centuries in England was considered totally socially acceptable.

book is an excellent source for more detailed information on this sadistic aspect of breed development. Suffice it to say that the most debasing act that this now most gentle of breeds had to perform was to attempt to tear its brother limb from limb to the joyous encouragement of the assembled "patrons of the sport."

The Bulldog is first mentioned in literature in the sixteenth century. "Bondogge," or "Banndogge," were used in 1576, while Shakespeare in his play *King Henry VI* refers to the "Bandog." Apparently it is questionable that the previous spellings bear any relationship to the actual Bulldog. In fact, breed historians (of the 1900s) totally disassociate the Bandog from the Bulldog, claiming that they were separate and distinct breeds. The Bandog was rough-coated and yellowish or sandy-gray in color; he also possessed keen scenting ability, which is a distinctly rare attribute in a well-conformed Bulldog. The Bandog was said to have resulted from a cross between the Mastiff and the Foxhound, hence the keen sense of smell. There is ample evidence, however, that the Bulldog has been used throughout the development of modern breeds to heighten the courage and improve the tenacity of a variety of other breeds. Over the centuries writers have come to different conclusions as to the origin of the Bulldog. Some have opined that the Bulldog and the Mastiff shared common parentage and were descended from the Alaunt, a kind of ancient Mastiff which is mentioned in Chaucer's *Canterbury Tales*. Buffon, a famous artist of his time, was emphatic that the Mastiff was the result of a cross between the Irish Wolfhound and the Bulldog. Many others disagreed with Buffon's position. In the very early history of British dogs, we are taught that the ancient Britons went into battle accompanied by large, ferocious dogs. Picture the hand-to-hand combat of these primeval warriors, legs totally unprotected, with these huge dogs armored with leather that bore sharp outward projections. It has been said that these dogs caused the Romans to don leggings as protection in battle.

In all probability the English Mastiff and the Bulldog are both descended from these ancient war dogs. All of the foregoing notwithstanding, we can still only guess at the true origin of the modern version of the Bulldog.

Shortly after bullbaiting became illegal and the Bulldog had fallen into disrepute because of his brutal past, there developed a real danger that this unique breed would die out altogether. Fortunately, a few hardy souls stepped forward and saved this breed that was so much a part of the history and culture of his homeland. His courage was proverbial and his character indomitable. No dog, however great, would ever overwhelm him; he would bear with unflinching heroism any pain to which he might be subjected.

From his bullbaiting associations, the Bulldog had the reputation of being a vicious, ferocious brute, but that was not his doing. Rather the responsibility lies squarely at the feet of his old-time master, who was not fit to be in the presence of this most dignified and gentle dog.

Those who rescued the Bulldog from extinction no longer wanted a ferocious killer, but they desired to retain the other qualities for which the breed was also renowned. They aimed to preserve the loyal, dignified, courageous dog that could be gentle and loving with the right owners but also mirror the bravery of his ancient ancestors.

The Bulldog that is familiar to us today is a far cry from the dog of two hundred years ago. In the early 1800s a Captain Thomas Brown wrote:

> . . . the Bulldog is low in stature, deep chested and strongly made about the shoulders and thighs, the muscles of both of which are extremely developed. His head is broad, his nose short and the underjaw projects beyond the upper, which gives him a fierce and disagreeable aspect. His eyes are distant and prominent and have a peculiar suspicious-like leer, which, with the distention of his nostrils, gives him a contemptuous look, and from the teeth always being seen, he has the constant appearance of grinning, while he is perfectly passive . . . but the most important quality . . . is the diminution of the brain. The cerebral capacity of the Bull-dog is sensibly smaller than in any other race, and it is doubtless to the decrease of the encephalon that we must attribute its inferiority to all others in everything relating to intelligence. The Bulldog is scarcely capable of any education and is fitted for nothing but combat and ferocity.

What say those of you that have Bulldogs with advanced obedience degrees?

In the early 1800s engravings of Bulldogs such as "Tumbler" and "Bess" depicted a very close resemblance to our modern Bulldogs, but their conformation suggested that they were extremely active as compared to

Ben White running his Bulldog, "Tumbler" and Lady Sandwich's "Bess" at the head of Bill Gibbons's bull, from a painting by J.C. Scanlan (circa 1836).

the Bulldog of today. There was the same great depth of chest, and extension of underjaw and muscular and powerful forelegs, with comparatively light hindquarters. The tails of these dogs were of a type that is seldom seen today, smooth and tapered, almost reaching to the hocks. To quote Henry St. John Cooper in 1900:

> The tail does not always commend itself to modern breeders, who, unfortunately, especially in the United States of America, are far too strongly in favor of the twist or screw tail, which is not, and never was a proper appendage of the Bulldog.

The major difference of that time and today is that the skull was too small in proportion to the size of the dog. The nose was somewhat long and the underjaw, though prominent, did not have that determined up-sweep that is regarded as one of the most important Bulldog attributes in the modern dog. The wrinkle covering the head was noticeably absent as compared to what we expect of our show dogs of today. We must not lose sight of the fact that these dogs were not meant to appear in beauty contests; they were specifically developed to be fighting dogs.

"Ball," owned by a Mr. Lovell, was given as an example of a nearly perfect Bulldog tail in Philo Kuon Standard.

The original Standard was taken from the embodiment of two highly regarded specimens of their time, "Crib" and "Rosa," circa 1817. Today it is highly unlikely that even the greenest novice to the breed would consider purchasing a specimen that resembled either of these "roadmarkers." However, "from small acorns, great oak trees grow." It is reported that they both mirrored a splendid type of active, capable dog possessing great chest capacity, strength and muscularity of neck. They also had neatly placed, low tail sets and perfection of the roach back. At the end of the twentieth century, responsible Bulldog breeders still try to breed for those essential attributes of breed type.

The first dog club to attempt to standardize any dog breed was what ultimately became the Bulldog Club. This same group also held the first conformation dog show on record, before the Kennel Club (England) was founded. Member breeders and owners even challenged their colleagues to long-distance "Bulldog walking contests," for a small wager, of course!

The first Standard of the Bulldog was the Philo Kuon, adopted in London in February 1865. The primary purpose of this document was to maintain a medium-sized dog of about fifty to fifty-five pounds, but sixty pounds was apparently acceptable. At the time the "rage" was to import very large, heavy, unhealthy, cumbersome dogs from Spain. Blessedly, the Standard was adhered to, however loosely, and it is rare today in the United States or Great Britain to see good Bulldogs that are much larger than the size given in the original Standard. Curiously, it seems to be currently fashionable in Asian countries to import dogs that meet the Spanish criteria of days of yore.

Many Bulldogs being shown in England before the turn of the twentieth century were exaggerated, unhealthy, crippled specimens. Their appearance caused an uprising of the "rank and file faithful," mainly the working-class fanciers of London, Birmingham, Sheffield and Nottingham, and a few other districts of England. It is to these dedicated breeders that we owe the existence of the Bulldog as we know it today. They were the source of "under the kitchen table" dogs

Sunday Evening with the Fancy (*probably mid–nineteenth century*).

that were bred not for profit, but for the sheer love of the breed. They were the truest, most dedicated type of dog fanciers of which it is possible to conceive.

Slowly but surely the Bulldog came back into popularity, not as a fighting dog, but primarily as a family pet that would occasionally be exhibited in the showring because of the love and pride his owners had for him.

The Bulldog's undesirable ferocity and savagery naturally disappeared, but early breeders, operating with a vague breed Standard, tended to breed for the exaggerations. Eventually they produced the progenitor of the Bulldog that we have today. The Standard demanded a large head, so they bred to get the head larger. The Standard required a great width of chest with short, muscular forelegs that were also sturdy and straight, so they bred for shorter, wider proportions. The writers of the 1900s tell us that it was not uncommon to see unfortunate animals with splay-feet and terribly bowed legs waddling helplessly around the ring, scarcely able to carry the weight of their own heads. Such truly grotesque creatures could never attack a bull or have the stamina to perform the breed's formerly required duties. The fanciers of the day were almost as cruel as the butchers of past centuries, as they designed contraptions with weights to force puppies lower to the ground and force their fronts to spread.

Eventually, earnest Bulldog enthusiasts of the late nineteenth century deluged the canine press in Britain, demanding that the national breed be allowed to return to a commonsense Standard, resulting in a dog that would be healthy and sound and naturally free of the gross exaggerations that were gaining ever greater acceptance; these concerned people demanded a balanced Bulldog. This was the forerunner of the modern Bulldog as we know it.

It is said that about 2 percent of those who are approved to judge truly understand the Bulldog and his physical idiosyncrasies. Those who make the conscious decision to seek approval to judge do so because they love dogs and the dog sport, and wish to positively impact purebred dogs in general and the breed or breeds of their greatest interest in particular. They have worked and studied extensively over an extended period so that, as judges, they can consistently make informed decisions under the pressure of actual competition.

"Lucy," from an engraving by Pyall, published 1834.

With particular emphasis on the Bulldog, it is more the rule than the exception that when an individual without a personal background in the breed officiates at a show the day before or after a breeder-judge does the honors, even the lower placements will not include the same dogs. Although this is generally true for any breed, it is more the case for breeds perceived as being more *esoteric*. This serves as a plausible explanation for so many dogs attaining their championships without ever having been awarded a single point from a breeder-judge, even though their owners or handlers have tried on numerous occasions to do so. It also accounts for why so many of these same dogs then go on to win numerous Bests of Breed and Group placements under all-breed and multiple-breed judges without actual experience with Bulldogs.

The Bulldog fan can ask a host of challenging questions to gain a better understanding of conditions within the breed. Why, for example, does the gallery feel more comfortable when a judge places dogs of an even size or the same color? Does this by itself really indicate consistency in judging? What are the upper and lower limits of size according to the Bulldog Standard and what is the ideal? Why might some neophyte Bulldog judges favor certain colors over others? Will a lack of self-confidence lead some judges to favor a professional handler or a

11

well-known breeder-exhibitor? Why do lame dogs sometimes win, even though the AKC rules explicitly forbid them to be shown? How can a Bulldog that naturally does not possess a tail win? Many Bulldogs win that present "anal confrontation" when viewed from above. Bulldogs with hound ears win. Bulldogs with scissor bites win, and so the list goes on. What are the reasons for this? Obviously the Bulldog Standard is difficult to interpret, even for breeders. Every Bulldog enthusiast will have their own personal likes and dislikes. However, it is not up to us to remake the Bulldog. Every breeder and every judge shares the obligation to the Bulldog to breed to the Standard that has stood the test of time, basically unchanged. If we, as a fancy, deviate from the Standard, then can the dogs we breed, show and judge truthfully be called Bulldogs?

Judges bear much of the responsibility for the breeding of poor specimens. When untypical Bulldogs win, a certain percentage will be bred and are likely to increase the population of faulty specimens. Judges can totally change the perception of what a good dog should be by questionable, inexpert judging. Those who have witnessed the decline of quality in a whole host of breeds know how important good judging is to maintaining quality in Bulldogs or in any other breed.

2

The Official Standard
of the Bulldog

GENERAL APPEARANCE

The Perfect Bulldog must be of medium size and smooth coat, with a heavy, thick-set, low-slung body, massive short-faced head, wide shoulders and sturdy limbs. The general appearance and attitude should suggest great stability, vigor and strength. The disposition should be equable and kind, resolute and courageous (not vicious or aggressive), and demeanor should be pacific and dignified. These attributes should be countenanced by the expression and behavior.

SIZE, PROPORTION, SYMMETRY

Size—The size for mature dogs is about fifty pounds, for mature bitches about forty pounds.

Proportion—The circumference of the skull in front of the ears should measure at least the height of the dog at the shoulders.

Symmetry—The "points" should be well distributed and bear good relation one to the other, no feature being in such prominence from either excess or lack of quality that the animal appears deformed or ill-proportioned.

Influence of Sex—In comparison of specimens of different sex, due allowance should be made in favor of the bitches, which do not bear the characteristics of the breed to the same degree of perfection and grandeur as do the dogs.

HEAD

Eyes and Eyelids—The eyes, seen from the front, should be situated low down in the skull, as far from the ears as possible, and their corners should be in a straight line at right angles with the stop. They should be quite in front of the head, as wide apart as possible, provided their outer corners are within the outline of the cheeks when viewed from the front. They should be round in form, of moderate size, neither sunken nor bulging and in color should be very dark. The lids should cover the white of the eyeball when the dog is looking directly forward, and the lid should show no "haw."

Ears—The ears should be set high on the head, the front inner edge of each ear joining the outline of the skull at the top back corner of the skull, so as to place them as wide apart, as high and as far from the eyes as possible. In size they should be small and thin. The shape termed "rose ear" is the most desirable. The rose ear folds inward at its back lower edge, the upper front edge curving over, outward and backward, showing part of the inside of the burr. (The ears should not be carried erect or prick-eared or buttoned and should never be cropped.)

Skull—The skull should be very large, and in circumference, in front of the ears, should measure at least the height of the dog at the shoulders. Viewed from the front, it should appear very high from the corner of the lower jaw to the apex of the skull, and also very broad and square. Viewed at the side, the head should appear very high, and very short from the point of the nose to occiput. The forehead should be flat (not rounded or domed), neither too prominent nor overhanging the face.

Cheeks—The cheeks should be well-rounded, protruding sideways and outward beyond the eyes.

Stop—The temples or frontal bones should be very well defined, broad, square and high, causing a hollow or groove between the eyes. This indentation, or stop, should be both broad and deep and extend up the middle of the forehead, dividing the head vertically, being traceable to the top of the skull.

Face and Muzzle—The face, measured from the front of the cheekbone to the tip of the nose, should be extremely short, the muzzle being very short, turned upward and very deep from the corner of the eye to the corner of the mouth.

Nose—The nose should be large, broad and black, its tip set back deeply between the eyes. The distance from bottom of stop, between the eyes, to the tip of nose should be as short as possible and not exceed the length from the tip of nose to the edge of underlip. The nostrils should be wide, large and black, with a well-defined line between them. Any nose other than black is objectionable and a brown or liver-colored nose shall *disqualify*.

Lips—The chops or "flews" should be thick, broad, pendant and very deep, completely overhanging the lower jaw at each side. They join the underlip in front and almost or quite cover the teeth, which should be scarcely noticeable when the mouth is closed.

Bite—*Jaws*—The jaws should be massive, very broad, square and "undershot," the lower jaw projecting considerably in front of the upper jaw and turning up.

Teeth—The teeth should be large and strong, with the canine teeth, or tusks, wide apart, and the six small teeth in front, between the canines, in an even, level row.

NECK, TOPLINE, BODY

Neck—The neck should be short, very thick, deep and strong and well arched at the back.

Topline—There should be a slight fall in the back, close behind the shoulders (its lowest part), whence the spine should rise to the loins (the top of which should be higher than the top of the shoulders), thence curving again more suddenly to the tail, forming an arch (a very distinctive feature of the breed), termed "roach back" or, more correctly, "wheel back."

Body—The brisket and body should be very capacious, with full sides, well-rounded ribs and very deep from the shoulders down to its lowest part, where it joins the chest. It should be well let down between the shoulders and forelegs, giving the dog a broad, low, short-legged appearance.

Chest—The chest should be very broad, deep and full.

Underline—The body should be well ribbed up behind, with the belly tucked up and not rotund. *Back and Loin*—The back should be short and strong, very broad at the shoulders and comparatively narrow at the loins.

Tail—The tail may be either straight or "screwed" (but never curved or curly), and in any case must be short, hung low, with decided downward carriage, thick root and fine tip. If straight, the tail should be cylindrical and of uniform taper. If "screwed," the bends or kinks should be well defined, and may be abrupt or even knotty, but no portion of the member should be elevated above the base or root.

FOREQUARTERS

Shoulders—The shoulders should be muscular, very heavy, widespread and slanting outward, giving stability and great power.

Forelegs—The forelegs should be short, very stout, straight and muscular, set wide apart with well-developed calves, presenting a bowed outline, but the bones of the legs should not be curved or bandy, nor the feet brought too close together.

Elbows—The elbows should be low and stand well out and loose from the body.

Feet—The feet should be moderate in size, compact and firmly set. Toes compact, well split up, with high knuckles and very short, stubby nails. The front feet may be straight or slightly turned out.

HINDQUARTERS

Legs—The hind legs should be strong and muscular and longer than the forelegs, so as to elevate the loins above the shoulders. Hocks should be slightly bent and well let down, so as to give length and strength from the loins to hock. The lower leg should be short, straight and strong, with the stifles turned slightly outward and away from the body. The hocks are thereby made to approach each other, and the hind feet to turn outward.

Feet—The feet should be moderate in size, compact and firmly set. Toes compact, well split up, with high knuckles and short, stubby nails. The hind feet should be pointed well outward.

COAT AND SKIN

Coat—The coat should be straight, short, flat, close, of fine texture, smooth and glossy. (No fringe, feather or curl.)

Skin—The skin should be soft and loose, especially at the head, neck and shoulders.

Wrinkles and Dewlap—The head and face should be covered with heavy wrinkles, and at the throat, from jaw to chest, there should be two loose pendulous folds, forming the dewlap.

COLOR OF COAT

The color of coat should be uniform, pure of its kind and brilliant. The various colors found in the breed are to be preferred in the following order: (1) red brindle, (2) all other brindles, (3) solid white, (4) solid red, fawn or fallow, (5) piebald, (6) inferior qualities of all the foregoing. *Note:* A perfect piebald is preferable to a muddy brindle or defective solid color. Solid black is very undesirable, but not so objectionable if occurring to a moderate degree in piebald patches. The brindles to be perfect should have a fine, even and equal distribution of the composite colors. In brindles and solid colors a small white patch on the chest is not considered detrimental. In piebalds the color patches should be well defined, of pure color and symmetrically distributed.

GAIT

The style and carriage are peculiar, his gait being a loose-jointed, shuffling, sidewise motion, giving the characteristic "roll." The action must, however, be unrestrained, free and vigorous.

TEMPERAMENT

The disposition should be equable and kind, resolute and courageous (not vicious or aggressive), and demeanor should be pacific and dignified. These attributes should be countenanced by the expression and behavior.

SCALE OF POINTS

General Properties			*Body, Legs, etc.*	
Proportion and			Neck	3
symmetry	5		Dewlap	2
Attitude	3		Shoulders	5
Expression	2		Chest	3
Gait	3		Ribs	3
Size	3		Brisket	2
Coat	2		Belly	2
Color of coat	4	<u>22</u>	Back	5

SCALE OF POINTS

Head			Forelegs and elbows	4	
Skull	5		Hind legs	3	
Cheeks	2		Feet	3	
Stop	4		Tail	4	<u>39</u>
Eyes and eyelids	3				
Ears	5				
Wrinkle	5				
Nose	6				
Chops	2				
Jaws	5				
Teeth	2	<u>39</u>	Total		100

DISQUALIFICATION

Brown or liver-colored nose.

Approved July 20, 1976
Reformatted November 28, 1990

CHAPTER

3

The Original British Standard with Historic Commentary

STANDARD AND DESCRIPTION OF THE CORRECT APPEARANCE AND THE several points in detail of a Perfectly-formed Bulldog, as adopted by The Bulldog Club (Incorporated). The following description of the Purebred Old English Bulldog has been compiled by The Bulldog Club (1875), as the correct standard type of excellence in the breed, after carefully obtaining all obtainable opinions.

In forming a judgment of any specimen of the breed, the general appearance—which is the first impression the dog makes as a whole on the eye of a judge—should be first considered. Secondly should be noticed its size, shape, and make, or rather its proportions in the relation they bear to each other. (No point should be so much in excess of the others as to destroy the general symmetry, or make the dog appear deformed, or interfere with its powers of motion, etc.) Thirdly, his style, carriage, gait, temper, and his several points should be considered

English Ch. Roseville Blaze, owned by George Woolon, is considered by most authorities one of the all-time greats of the breed.

separately in detail, as follows, due allowance being made for the bitch, which is not so grand or as well developed as the dog:

1. The general appearance of the Bulldog is that of a smooth coated, thick-set dog, rather low in stature, but broad, powerful and compact. Its head strikingly massive, and large in proportion to the dog's size. Its face extremely short. Its muzzle very broad, blunt and inclined upwards. Its body short and well-knit; the limbs stout and muscular. Its hind quarters very high and strong, but rather lightly made in comparison with its heavily made foreparts. The dog conveys an impression of determination, strength, and activity, similar to that suggested by the appearance of a thick-set Ayrshire or Highland bull.

2. The skull should be very large—the larger the better—and in circumference should measure (round in front of the ears) at least the height of the dog at the shoulders. Viewed from the front, it should appear very high from the corner of the lower jaw to the apex of the

skull, and also very broad and square. The cheeks should be well rounded and extend sideways beyond the eyes. Viewed at the side, the head should appear very high, and very short from its back to the point of the nose. The forehead should be flat, neither prominent nor overhanging the face; and the skin upon it and about the head very loose, hanging in large wrinkles.

3. The temples or frontal bones should be very prominent, broad, square and high, causing a deep and wide groove between the eyes. This indentation is termed the "stop," and should be both broad and deep, and extend up the middle of the forehead, dividing the head vertically, being traceable at the top of the skull.

4. The eyes, seen from the front, should be situated low down in the skull, as far from the ears as possible. Their corners should be in a straight line at right angles with the stop, and quite in front with the head. They should be wide apart as possible, provided their outer corners are within the outline of the cheeks. They should be quite round in shape, of moderate size, neither sunken nor prominent, and in color should be very dark—almost, if not quite black, showing no white when looking directly forward.

5. The ears should be set high in the head—*i.e.*, the front inner edge of each ear should (as viewed from the front) join the outline of the skull at the top corner of such outline, so as to place them as wide apart, and as high and as far from the eyes as possible. In size they should be small and thin. The shape termed "rose ear" is the most correct. The "rose ear" folds inwards at its back, the upper or front edge curving over outwards and backwards, showing part of the inside of the burr.

6. The face, measured from the front of the cheekbone to the nose, should be as short as possible, and its skin should be deeply and closely wrinkled. The muzzle should be short, broad, turned upwards, and very deep from the corner of the eye to the corner of the mouth. The nose should be large, broad and black; its top should be deeply set back, almost between the eyes. The distance from the inner corner of the eye (or from the centre of the stop between the eyes) to the extreme tip of the nose should not exceed the length from the tip of the nose to the edge of the underlip. The nostrils

should be large, wide and black, with a well-defined straight line between them.

7. The flews, called the "chop," should be thick, broad, pendant and very deep, hanging completely over the lower jaw at the sides (not in front). They should join the underlip in front, and quite cover the teeth, which should not be seen when the mouth is closed.

8. The jaw should be broad, massive and square, the canine teeth, or tusks, wide apart. The lower jaw should project considerably in front of the upper and turn up. It should be broad and square, and have the six small front teeth between the canines in an even row. The teeth should be large and strong.

9. The neck should be moderate in length (rather short than long), very thick, deep and strong. It should be well arched at the back, with much loose, thick, and wrinkled skin about the throat, forming a dewlap on each side, from the lower jaw to the chest. The chest should be very wide laterally, round, prominent and deep, making the dog appear very broad and short-legged in front.

10. The shoulders should be broad, slanting and deep, very powerful and muscular.

11. The brisket should be capacious, round and very deep from the top of the shoulders to its lowest part where it joins the chest, and be well let down between the forelegs. It should be large in diameter, and round behind the forelegs (not flat sided, the ribs being well rounded). The body should be well ribbed up behind, with the belly tucked up, and not pendulous.

12. The back should be short and strong, very broad at the shoulder, and comparatively narrow at the loins. There should be a slight fall to the back close behind the shoulders (its lowest part), whence the spine should rise to the loins (the top of which should be higher than the top of the shoulders), thence curving again more suddenly to the tail, forming an arch—a distinctive characteristic of the breed termed "roach-back," or more correctly "wheel-back."

13. The tail, termed the "stern," should be set on low, jut out rather straight, then turn downwards, the end pointing horizontally. It should be quite round in its own length, smooth and devoid of fringe or coarse hair. It should be moderate in length—rather short than

long—thick at the root, and tapering quickly to a fine point. It should have a downward carriage (not having a decided upward curve at the end or being screwed or deformed), and the dog should, from its shape, not be able to raise it over its back.

14. The forelegs should be very stout and strong, set wide apart, thick, muscular and straight, with well-developed calves presenting a rather bowed outline, but the bones of the legs should be large and straight, not bandy or curved. They should be rather short in proportion to the hind legs, but not so short as to make the back appear long or detract from the dog's activity, and so cripple him. The elbows should be low, and stand well away from the ribs. The ankles, or pasterns, should be short, straight and strong. The forefeet should be straight, and turn very slightly outward, of medium size and moderately round. The toes compact and thick, being well split up, making the knuckles prominent and high.

15. The hind legs should be large and muscular, and longer in proportion than the forelegs, so as to elevate the loins. The hocks should be slightly bent and well let down, so as to be long and muscular from the loins to the point of the hock. The lower part of the leg should be short, straight and strong. The stifles should be round, and turned slightly outwards away from the body. The hocks are thereby made to approach each other, and the hind feet to turn outwards. The latter, like the forefeet, should be round and compact, with the toes well split up and the knuckles prominent. From his formation the dog has a peculiar heavy, and constrained gait, appearing to walk with short quick steps on the tip of his toes, his hind feet not being lifted high, but appearing to skim the ground, and running with the right shoulder advanced, similar to the manner of a horse in cantering.

16. The most desirable size for the Bulldog is about 50 lbs.

17. The coat should be fine in texture, short, close and smooth (hard only from its shortness and closeness, not wiry). Its color should be whole or smut (that is, a whole color with a black mask or muzzle). The colors in their order of merit, if bright and pure, are, first, whole colors and smuts—viz. brindles, reds, white, with their varieties, as whole fawns, fallows, etc.; second, pied and mixed colors.

THE PERFECT BULLDOG—A GUIDE FOR EXHIBITORS, BREEDERS AND JUDGES

by J. Hay Hutchinson (1908)

Introduction

In this work I have attempted in pictorial diagrams to present in a way that can be readily understood the various defects in modern Bulldogs, and I have placed alongside these other diagrams showing the ideal points as laid down in the descriptions and standard of points of the several Bulldog clubs. My excuse for undertaking this task is that, while most authorities are agreed on the subject in theory, their interpretations are as diverse as those of art critics, and this I believe to be largely due to the fact that the works on the Bulldog have hitherto been confined to written descriptions and discussions, without the necessary illustrative sketches to show the points in a clear and unmistakable manner. I believe my sketches will demonstrate not only the defects, but also the qualities desired in this noble breed of dog in a more intelligible manner than has hitherto been attempted. I may add that my study of the Bulldog—which has extended over a period of twenty years—has led me to the conclusion that the perfect Bulldog of today should, though it is not called on to exhibit its prowess in the field, be the embodiment in appearance at least of the activity, strength and endurance that go to make a dog capable of bullbaiting. The greater humanity of modern times has stamped out the old sport of baiting bulls or bears, and the Bulldog itself would no doubt have become as extinct as the dodo, but for its cult by enthusiastic fanciers. That it still retains its old historic instincts is not doubted by those who are thoroughly conversant with the subject, and modern instances of its capabilities when aroused are plentiful. The scientific efforts which have been brought to bear on its breeding have made the ideal Bulldog quite as capable as its predecessors. The only element lacking is that of the training by use to its special kinds of work, and of course, disuse in any department of animal activity means temporary unfitness. But the present-day Bulldog's wide chest, short nose and light hindquarters have all their obvious meaning, and its qualities of dour, determined pluck are indubitable. The ideal Bulldog that I have essayed to portray is the symmetrical, well-proportioned and active dog, free from exaggeration and monstrosity.

I shall be glad if my illustrations lead to a more clearly defined knowledge of the essential points to be looked for in the perfect specimen, and of the faults to be avoided.

THE HEAD

Skull and Foreface

Although it is generally known that the Bulldog should possess a large skull and massive foreface, it is not altogether clear to many what constitutes the correct shape of skull and correct formation of foreface. A Bulldog may sometimes have a skull that from the point of view of size may be all that is desired, but at the same time be so unshapely as to amount to a disfigurement, or he may have a large skull tolerably good in its proportions and outline, but so lacking in the finish as to defeat his chances of ranking as a first-rate specimen of the breed. In foreface, as well, a dog may be sufficently massive, and even may be possessed of sufficient "lay-back" and yet fall short of good conformation. The accompanying diagrams are arranged with the view to show as clearly as possible the qualities necessary for the perfect conformation of skull and foreface, also some common defects.

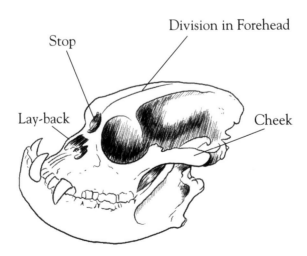

Figure 1.

Figure 1 shows a side view of the complete skull, which will probably help to give a clearer idea of the various qualities that produce the desired finish than could be shown by a view of the head itself.

Figure 2.

Figure 2 shows the undesirable domed or "apple-head" in conjunction with a well-formed foreface. Here the groove, the temples and the cheek are without clear definition. There is a want of squareness along the temples or frontal bones, destroying the effect of clear-cut finish in the skull. The foreface has the desired squareness and massiveness. The muzzle is short, broad and turned upward. The breadth and squareness of the foreface depend, in a great measure, on the width between and position of the canine teeth of the lower jaw (see Figure 1). When these teeth are narrowly placed there cannot be squareness of the foreface, as they can act as a prop, or support, to the so-called cushion. It may also be noted here that the nose is large and wide, but not strikingly out of line with the lay-back. Where the lay-back approaches a perfect line, it is seldom or never accompanied by the desired large nose and open nostril.

Figure 3.

Figure 3 shows a well-formed skull in conjunction with a deficient fore-face. Here the skull is large, long, broad and square, with the groove, temples and cheek well defined, and the stop deep and broad. The fore-face is small and weak in construction.

Figure 4.

Figure 4 shows the outline of the perfect head, with a due balance of the proportion between skull and foreface.

THE UNDERJAW

How often at the various Bulldog shows one hears a dog commended for his "wonderful underjaw"? As this is usually remarked about an animal probably possessing the overprominent, straight and long jaw, it shows there is some confusion in the mind of the average Bulldog admirer of what constitutes the correct formation. The Bulldog Club Inc., in its excellent description of the correct appearance of the Bulldog, referring to this point, says: "The jaws should be broad, massive and square, the canine teeth, or tusks, wide apart. The lower jaw should project considerably in front of the upper, and turn up. It should be broad and square, and have six small front teeth between the canines in an even row."

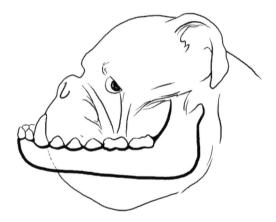

Figure 1.

This is good, as far as it goes, but is not sufficiently defined to make the matter quite clear. The ideal bronze model of the perfect specimen according to the Bulldog Club shows correctly what is required. Unfortunately, the majority of the Bulldog fraternity do not have the opportunity of inspecting this model, and to those the accompanying diagrams may prove welcome, as helping to make clear the correct type of jaw. Figure 1 shows the overprominent, long and straight jaw, with the canines exposed. This type, though often seen in connection with good breadth of jaw, is usually accompanied by want of depth through the face.

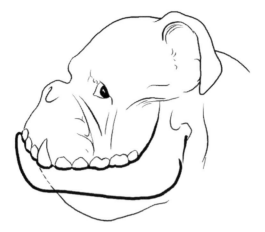

Figure 2.

Figure 2 is also a straight jaw, having the turn-up only at the extreme front. This is perhaps a worse type than shown in Figure 1, usually having a tendency to get narrow and pinched in front, and is more readily confounded with the correct type.

Figure 3.

Figure 3. This is the better type, calling for the closest observation to distinguish it from the correct type. This is the jaw with the straight upward thrust, but entirely lacking in the much desired curved turn-up. Figure 4 shows the correct type, so eagerly sought after in the fancy, with the upward thrust, and retaining the curve throughout.

It will be seen from these diagrams that it is not quite an easy matter to distinguish the correct type. Take for instance, a dog in Figure 3 as he appears on the show bench.

Figure 4.

Viewed from the front, his appearance would readily deceive even the more experienced of the fancy, but on a closer inspection of the mouth it would be immediately apparent, by the setting of the teeth, that the jaw was a straight one. In fact, a careful examination of the mouth is always essential where one wishes to be satisfied of the actual formation of the jaw.

THE EARS

In consideration of the discussion that has taken place on the question raised by the Kennel Club, whether the "tulip" ears should be a disqualification for a Bulldog, the accompanying diagrams of the ear carriage may prove of interest.

These diagrams help to show how much the ear carriage affects the expression of the head.

Figure 1. This ear carriage was common among the old-time Bulldogs in the Bullbaiting days, as may be seen from many of the old prints of the period. This was undoubtedly the form of the ear of the dog in his wild state, before he came in contact with civilization. Wild animals invariably have this form of ear.

Figure 1. The Erect Ear.

Figure 2. This may be said to be the first stage of development of the "rose" ear, and (according to the old prints) this was the prevailing form among the bullbaiting dogs. Though undeveloped from the modern point of view, it cannot be said to have any suspicion of malformation.

Figure 3. This cannot be said to be an undeveloped ear, and it may not be malformed; but the carriage of the ear is so much at variance with the requirements of the modern standard, and its effect so detrimental to the expression of the dog, that it practically may be considered as a malformation. Falling, as it does, across the head, it not only has the effect of diminishing the apparent size of the skull, but quite destroys the expression of an otherwise fine head.

Figure 2. The "Tulip" Ear.

Figure 3. The "Button" Ear.

Figure 4. This is the standard form of ear that fulfills the requirements of the modern standard, and is undoubtedly the form that sets off to the best advantage the head of the Bulldog. Its lines are in harmony with those of the skull, and it has the effect of increasing the size of the skull without in any way interfering with the alert expression of the dog.

Figure 4. The "Rose" Ear.

THE EXPRESSION

The question of whether the modern Bulldog is lacking in expression is one that is the cause of considerable discussion. Considering the difficulty of giving a clear definition of the desirable Bulldog expression, it is not to be wondered that there should be many and widely different views on the subject. By constant observation and comparison, one can arrive at an approximately accurate knowledge of the points of the breed, and be able to apply that knowledge to a given specimen, so far as to give a formal description, point by point, of the good qualities and the deficiencies; but there seem to be few who were able to treat the subtle subject of expression in this manner, and to state explicitly which qualities go to make or mar the expression. No doubt most of our Bulldog experts are able in an offhand manner to give a tolerably correct opinion whether a given specimen is possessed of, or lacking in the proper expression, but many of these would be at fault if called upon to give a more explicit opinion, and state clearly what are the qualities that go to perfect the expression, or to point out the deficiencies that tend to spoil it. Now, as the expression must necessarily depend entirely on the form and structural lines of the head and features, it should be possible—if our knowledge of the subject were not vague and superficial—to show exactly which lines and forms in the structure of the face produce a good or bad expression, or which deficiences cause want of expression.

Before attempting to show how these structural lines and forms affect the expression, it will be necessary to arrive at a clear understanding of the desirable or true expression of the Bulldog, as even on this subject there is considerable difference of opinion. On the one hand an expression, the dominant quality of which is, perhaps, ferocity, will be shown with pride as a fine typical Bulldog expression; on the other hand an expression of fawning amiability as the dominant quality will be similarly described.

Figure 1. Proportions of head good; expression good with the lines producing "sourness" emphasized.

The expression becomes molded to the nature, so—without taking into consideration in the meantime the influence of passion or emotion—a true expression is the outward and visible indication of the character and disposition. Fortunately, there is not this wide difference of opinion of what is desirable in the character and disposition of the ideal Bulldog, and we may safely assume that the desired characteristics are: courage, determination, tenacity, strength and activity, combined with intelligence, honesty and an even temper. Now, it follows that the true and desirable Bulldog expression is the one that most faithfully indicates *all* these characteristics.

Among Bulldog fanciers much stress is laid upon what, for want of a better word, is called "sourness" as a desirable quality in the expression. This has been described as the sourness of aloofness rather than the sourness of ill temper, a sourness that in a human being would probably be called haughtiness. A word more expressive of this quality is the Scottish "dourness," which comprehends in its meaning determination as well as "sourness," and is the very antithesis of all fawning and "gush."

Figure 2. Proportion of head the same as in Figure 1, but marred by large, badly carried ears; expression bad owing to eyes being narrowly placed and obliquely set; want of firmness in lower jaw, "stop" and temples badly defined and lines of expression bad throughout.

It is well that this sourness is considered an important quality in the expression, for if rightly understood it is the equivalent for courage, determination, tenacity and incidentally of strength in the expression, and should rank as the dominant quality. First, then, let us consider which lines are essential for producing this "sourness" of expression in the countenance of the Bulldog. The wide, deep "stop," accentuated by the prominent temples, with the furrow down the skull clearly defined; the well-broken-up face emphasizing the form of the foreface; the wide, well-turned-up underjaw, with the long downward sweep of the lines of the flews strongly and clearly marked, are the qualities that in themselves will produce the sour expression. But in association with these, the importance of the eye as a medium of expression must not be overlooked, and what would be considered the morose expression in the human eye is a near approach to what is required to perfect the sour expression of the eye in the Bulldog. The firmly marked upper eyelid with the curve slightly dipping into the eye produces this effect.

Figure 3. Proportions of foreface small compared to skull; expression deficient in strength.

But the eye itself and the placing of the eye are of such vital importance to the expression as to require special consideration. What we have called honesty as a characteristic of the Bulldog depends entirely for its expression on the eye, and the placing of the eyes. The eyes squarely set in the head and very wide apart are indicative of this quality. Nothing is more expressive of cunning than obliquely set eyes, narrowly placed. Again, the eye that shows much of the whites effectively destroys this expression of honesty. This defect is associated with that restlessness of eye, which is at once suggestive of treachery. Only when the animal is under strong excitement, with the eyelid drawn up and the eye dilated, should there be much of a show of the whites. Neither should the pupil be too light in color, as this tends to produce a similar effect to showing the whites. Thus it will be seen that for a proper expression the eyes require to be widely placed, squarely set, and dark in color; in addition, the size of the eye has to be taken into account. The small eye seriously affects the expression. On the other hand , the large "goggle" eye, usually associated with the "froggy" face, is thoroughly undesirable. The eye, to give true expression, should be large, but not prominent, and sufficiently wide open to admit of that sparkle so expressive of spirit, health and vitality.

In considering expression as an indication of strength and intelligence, it will be necessary to accurately observe the form and proportions of the whole head, as on the balance of proportion, between the skull and foreface depends the character of the head—the powerful foreface, with the small skull, expressing strength without intelligence; and the massive skull, with the puny foreface, expressing intelligence without strength. Shortness of muzzle and depth of face in front, where the canine teeth are situated, the large and wide turned-up underjaw, all have a powerful capacity for expressing strength. In the Bulldog, and indeed in all carnivorous animals, much of the character of the face lies in the depth of the jaw forward—a depth necessary for the socketing of the canine teeth.

In studying the mouth and jaw, we shall be readily convinced that the form and size of the bones are adapted to the necessities of the animal. Thus the jaws of the Bulldog, contrasted with the other parts of the face, should be exceptionally large, and any weakness or deficiency of this part is a serious defect. This is truly borne out in the expression, for nothing is more fatal to the appearance of strength in the face than the shallow foreface and weak receding underjaw. Breadth of face, giving room for the large muscle extending to the cheek, which closes the jaw, as well as the prominent cheek itself, are features important in giving conformity to the expression of strength.

The exposure of the canine teeth as an element in expression is certainly objectionable, and should be considered a defect, as it gives an undue air of ferocity and savageness, which cannot be sufficiently counteracted by any other feature, thus disturbing the balance of the expression to the loss of dignity. Only when the animal is in a state of excitement or rage, when the snarling muscles are brought into use, and the lips dragged back as a preliminary for the fangs to be used, should the canines be exposed. To give the perfect expression to the mouth the lips require to close tightly; and clumsiness or slackness here interferes with the long sweeping lines of the flews, and consequently weakens the expression of the lower jaw.

Figure 4. Proportions of foreface too large compared to skull; expression deficient in intelligence.

The nostrils are features that also have a powerful effect in giving not only spirit and vitality, but also strength to the expression. The nostrils may be said to indicate the state of the lungs; and the spirit of the open nostril is really the indication for the capacity for "wind."

It is in comparing the relative proportions of the head when we call into use that operation of the fancy, that associating power, which has the constant influence on our opinion, that a head in which the capacity of the skull is small, compared to the lower face, seems degraded and brutal. Thus an animal with a powerful development of lower face and jaw requires a corresponding development of the skull or brain capacity to avoid this degraded or brutal expression. By the massive proportions of his skull formation the Bulldog entirely avoids this expression, and on the contrary has a very evident expression of intelligence—even of nobleness and dignity—where the skull formation is perfect and nullified by no adjacent defect. The obtrusive or badly carried ear is one of the most common defects that mars this expression, as it tends to dwarf the apparent size of the skull, whereas the small, well-carried ear has an opposite effect.

Figure 5. "Frog face"—pinched foreface, weak underjaw and large, protruding eyes—giving a very undesirable effect to the expression.

The lines of the properly carried ear conform to, and thus emphasize, the outside lines of the skull, and have the effect of adding to its apparent size. To give the proper expression, it is of the first importance that the skull should have the appearance of massiveness, that is, great in its length, width and depth; and a certain squareness in the form gives an air of set maturity not otherwise obtained. "Wrinkle" is another feature that has to be considered in regard to the expression of the skull. Slackness of skin is certainly of advantage, and when the lines of the wrinkle conform to the contour of the skull they are of undoubted value in emphasizing the form; but when the wrinkle is overprofuse, or meaningless in line—regarded in association with the form of the head—or the lines so pronounced as to be effective in breaking up the appearance of mass of head, they are then of more than doubtful value in the expression. The quiet, dark eye, as an important feature in giving intelligence to the expression, must not be overlooked. Neither must it be forgotten that mobility of expression, so evident in the Bulldog, and, indeed, the capacity for strong expression itself, are marks of intelligence.

Figure 6. Proportions of the head and lines of expression the same as in Figure 1, but the features are excited in rage: the eyes and nostrils are dilated; the upper lip is drawn upward, producing a snarling effect and exposing the fangs.

For the expression of even temper, it will be necessary again to observe the balance of proportion of the head, the width between eyes and the eye itself. Narrowly placed eyes, showing of white, exposed canine teeth, deep markings at the lobes of the nose on the foreface or twitching of the upper lip are blemishes that tend to defeat the expression of even temper.

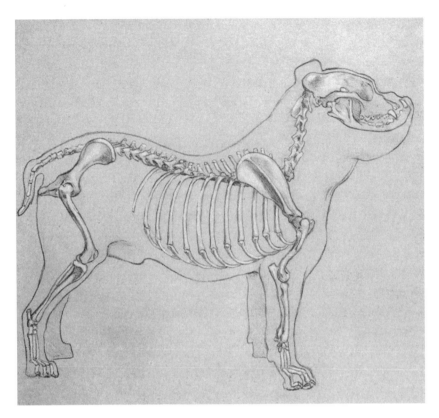

Skeleton of the Bulldog.—Enno Meyer

THE BODY

The Shoulders and Forelegs

In considering the body qualities of the Bulldog, the shoulder formation and front rank as of first importance. The great width of front is one of the distinctive characteristics of the breed, and is considered of so much importance among fanciers, that however perfect a dog may be in other respects, his failure in this one respect defeats his claim to high-class honors.

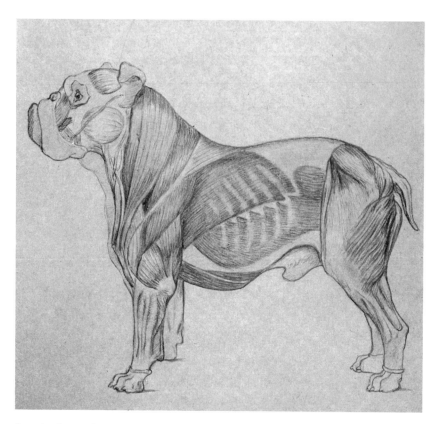

Superficial muscular system.—Enno Meyer

The beginner in the fancy will do well to make the consideration of this part his first care. It will be found that to be able to tell whether a dog is perfect in this respect is not such a simple matter as may appear at first glance, and there are many defects and malformations not easily discerned by the uninitiated. Wide placed forelegs are in themselves not all that is required of a good front; these may be badly formed or turned, placed on a very defective shoulder formation or the shoulders may be "tight" and the width be produced by misplacement at elbows. Again, it is not beyond suspicion that sometimes the wide front has been developed by artificial means in puppyhood by unscrupulous breeders.

In endeavoring to detect these defects the action of the animal is worthy of careful study, as it is unusual where there is a defect of the

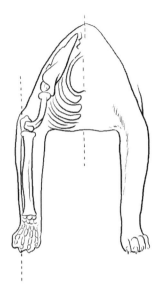

Figure 1. Fox Terrier front.

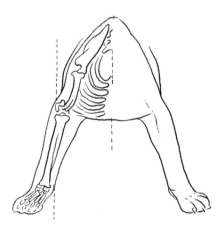

Figure 2. Same construction as Figure 1 (only forced).

shoulder formation for the dog to be possessed of that freedom of action seen in the perfect specimen.

The diagrams show some of the principal defects as well as the perfect conformation.

Figure 1 shows what is known as the Fox Terrier front. The legs are long and wanting in substance, and the shoulders tight. This form does not allow the width of chest so characteristic of the Bulldog, and necessary for the full development of the organs of the chest.

Figure 2 illustrates the same shoulder formation as Figure 1, the only difference being in the placing of the feet. Sometimes, by habit or training, a dog gets into this way of placing his feet, and is credited with a wider front than he really possesses.

Figure 3 shows a malformation usually associated with rickets. The shoulder formation is not sound, and the width is depending a great deal upon the elbow being unduly turned outward. The pasterns are turned too much inward, and the foot turned too much outward.

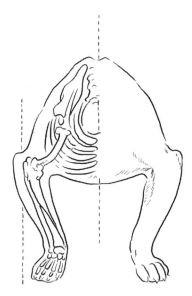

Figure 3. Extreme front.

Figure 4 shows an abnormal development of the width of front, inconsistent with strength or freedom of action. Where there is excessive width and bend in the bones of the forearm, there is always a suspicion that artificial means have been resorted to in early puppyhood to produce this result.

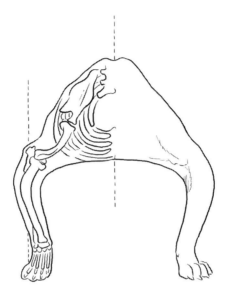

Figure 4. Artificially made front.

Figure 5 shows the perfect front with the correct placement and formation of shoulders. Here we have the width of front with slanting shoulders, great substance in limbs and depth of brisket combined with straightness of bone of the forearm, the necessary turn at elbow, and the feet placed with the toes turned slightly outward, giving firmness to the stand.

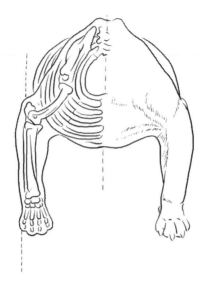

Figure 5. The perfect front.

Figure 6. The perfect front shown in conjunction with neck and head.

THE RIBS, CHEST AND LOIN

There is, perhaps, no line in the whole composition of the form of the Bulldog which is of more importance than that which gives the depth of chest and "tuck-up" of loin. In lines of construction it is a truism that fitness and beauty cannot be separated, and in no case is this more applicable than when considered anatomically. Chest development is of as great importance for strength and endurance to the animal as to the athlete, and flabbiness equally detrimental. Keeping this in mind, the great importance of the full development of this line will be allowed, for the depth of brisket, "tuck-up" at loin, and "spring" of rib are the outward symbols of lung power and activity; and no less surely are the shallow brisket, the flat sides, and pendulous belly associated with the feeble, listless and decadent specimen.

Figure 1.

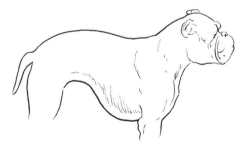

Figure 2.

In the showring, where it is impracticable to judge of a dog's fitness by tests of strength or endurance, it is surely of greater importance that the outward symbols of these qualities should receive their due share of attention, and no greater mistake is made at our shows than when a Bulldog, obviously deficient in these qualities, is awarded high honors, and nothing is more at variance with the true fancier's ideals.

Though the modern Bulldog is not called upon to emulate the deeds of his heroic ancestors, there is no reason why any of those obvious signs of feebleness or decadence should be tolerated in show specimens. On the contrary, the modern dog, with all the scientific attention that has been paid to his breeding and rearing, should—in appearance, at least—be the very embodiment of strength, endurance and activity.

The diagrams given here are arranged to show the desirable and undesirable form of brisket and "tuck-up" at loin, as well as the badly sprung rib. *Figure 1* shows the line of the shallow chest and brisket and the flabby, pendulous belly. It is out of the question to expect a dog thus poorly developed to be possessed of much strength or activity. The shallowness of brisket does not allow sufficent space for the full development of lungs and organs of the chest. The clumsiness or weight under loin interferes with the free action of the hindquarters, thus affecting the activity of the animal.

The whole line of the brisket and "tuck-up"—which ought to be one of the most beautiful lines of the animal—is rendered uninteresting and meaningless.

Figure 2 shows the line of the deep brisket well "tucked-up" at loin. The deep, capacious brisket allows ample room for full lung development. The clean cut-up at loin allows the fullest freedom to the hindquarters with the minimum of weight, and gives a line that at once stands for strength, activity and beauty combined.

Figure 3. Front view of the ribs in flat-sided, badly developed specimen. It will be seen here there is insufficient roundness or "spring" of the ribs.

Figure 4 shows another front view of the ribs in a well-developed specimen. The ribs are well-rounded or "sprung" at the fullest behind the shoulders, giving ample capacity for the full development of the organs of the chest. An animal with this formation will always give the direct impression of strength and power, never associated with flat sides and shallow brisket.

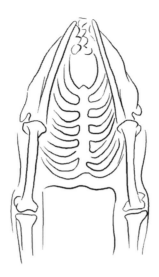

Figure 3.

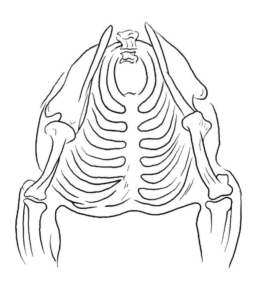

Figure 4.

THE BACK

In the evolution of the Bulldog from the earliest times to the present day there has been perhaps no single characteristic more distinctive of the breed than the "roach" or "wheel back." There cannot be the slightest doubt that this was a striking characteristic of the old-time dog. The prints of the period almost invariably show the dog perfect in this particular. Unfortunately, the same cannot be said about many of our present-day dogs. From the show bench point of view alone, this is a matter of serious regret, for nothing gives more gracefully the impression of activity and strength than do the beautiful lines of the "roach back." It is to be hoped that breeders are alive to this deficiency in the modern dog, and do their utmost to preserve those lines, so much beloved by admirers of the breed, particularly those of the "old school."

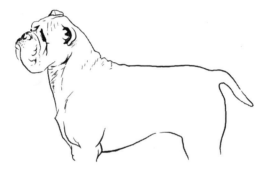

Figure 1.

These diagrams illustrate some of the imperfect forms of back, most common in the modern Bulldog, as well as the perfectly-formed "roach back."

Figure 1. The "straight back." However desirable in certain other breeds, this form is thoroughly undesirable in the Bulldog, anything in the nature of a straight line being utterly out of harmony with every other line of the dog. The "straight back" is necessarily accompanied by the high set-on tail.

Figure 2.

Figure 2. The "saddle" or "swamp back." Dogs having a tendency to be lengthy in back have often this form. This is undoubtedly a weak form, and is sometimes confounded by the novice with the "roach back"; but it will be observed that the line sinks with a rather sudden curve behind the wither, and is inclined to rise toward the stern.

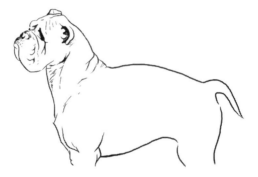

Figure 3.

Figure 3. The "arched" or "camel back." Even among the more discerning this form often passes as the genuine "roach back," and this is not surprising, as it sometimes takes the closest and most careful attention on the part of the observer to distinguish between the two. It will be noticed that the curve of the spine starts abruptly behind the wither, going with one sweep to the stern.

53

Figure 4.

Figure 4. The "roach" or "wheel back"—the perfect form. There is a slight fall to the back close behind the wither, whence the spine rises to the loins, thence curving again more suddenly to the stern.

THE HIND LEGS

In considering the merits of a Bulldog the forelegs and front are always likely to receive their full measure of attention, while anything short of an actual deformity in the hind legs is often passed over as of comparatively little importance. When it is considered that to a great degree the animal depends on the strength and formation of the hind legs for his activity, this a matter of no small wonder, especially so in the case of the Bulldog, in whom activity is so much to be desired. Again, it is in no small measure that the long graceful lines of the hock contribute to that nobility and elegance of appearance so much admired in the perfect specimen.

It will be my endeavor, by means of the accompanying diagrams, to point out a few of the more common defects in the hindquarters of the present day dog, and to show the construction of the limb that produces the desired appearance of elegance, strength and activity.

Figure 1 shows what is perhaps the most common defect of the hind leg, viz., the straight hock—not at all a pleasant formation when in repose, and giving a "stilted" effect to the action of the animal. It also affects the appearance of the foot, giving the effect of an upward thrust of the toes.

Figure 2 shows a malformation in the opposite direction to Figure 1. Here the bend of the hock is overpronounced, giving the appearance of

Figure 1.

Figure 2.

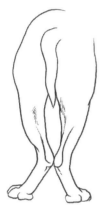

Figure 3.

Figure 4.

want of firmness to the "stand" of the animal, and is often accompanied by a weakness at the stifle and a hare foot.

Figure 3 shows a particularly ungainly formation known as the "cow-hock." Here the hock is turned too much inward, consequently the stifle and toes turn too much outward. This defect gives a shuffling effect to the action of the animal.

Figure 4 shows a dog with this malformation said to be "pigeon-toed." It is a defect in the opposite direction to that shown in Figure 3. Here we

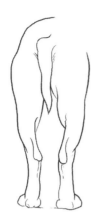

Figure 5.   Figure 6.

have the hock turned outward, causing the stifle and foot to turn inward. This also gives a very ungainly effect to the dog's action.

Figures 5 and 6 show the perfect formation from different points of view. In Figure 5 it will be seen that the hock is slightly turned inward, giving a slight outward turn to the stifle and foot. Figure 6 shows the perfect bend of the hock, with the long muscular lines from the loin to the point of the hock; the lower part of the leg is short, straight and strong.

THE FEET

In connection with the various points of a Bulldog, perhaps no minor point is more generally overlooked than the feet, and it is curious how few breeders there are who take the smallest trouble over this point. There can be no doubt that bad feet not only take away from the appearance of a dog, but do so much to impair his activity and vigor as to have a deleterious effect upon his general health. A Bulldog, to enjoy perfect health, should be able to romp and play as actively as a kitten, but this is impossible unless he is possessed of perfectly sound feet. It is surely time that this point was given more attention, considering that some of our prize dogs today could not be depended upon to walk half a mile of the road without being completely used up. From this point of view alone bad feet are a serious enough defect, as many a fancier knows from sad experience. It is no joke to have to pick up and carry for even a short distance a dog of the desired fifty-pound weight, a very undesirable weight under the circumstances! In Fox Terriers and other breeds the feet are considered a point of the first importance, and th₁ re is no reason why it should not be considered of equal importance in the case of the Bulldog. An animal with such a massive head and heavily constructed forequarters must nec-essarily require sound, compact and well-padded feet to support his weight. From the show-bench point of view many a dog with an otherwise shapely foreleg is spoiled by unsound or badly turned feet. As there has been lately some discussion in Bulldog circles on what really constitutes the correct formation of the Bulldog's foot, probably the accompanying diagrams will help to make this "point" better understood.

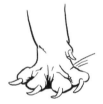

Figure 1.

Figure 1. This is the "splayed"or "duck foot." Here there is obviously a serious deficiency of strength in the muscles of the foot, causing wide spaces between the toes. This gives a very undesirable "sprawly" effect to the foot, even affecting the correct growth of the claws. This in itself is sufficient to cause the dog to be easily lamed, the claws not being in the proper opposition to afford the necessary protection to the toes. Taken altogether, a dog with feet of this formation makes a very poor attempt at running, and is quickly used up even in walking.

Figure 2.

Figure 2. The "hare foot" is another weak and undesirable form of foot, though not so unsightly as that shown in Figure 1. A dog with "hare feet" is usually also narrow-fronted, and often "down on pasterns" as well, and is incapable of doing much running or walking.

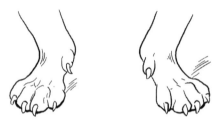

Figure 3.

Figure 3. The defect in this formation is more in the turn of foot and in the pasterns than in the foot itself. Though it is desirable and according to the club standard that the foot should have a slight outward turn, here we have it much overdone, and when this is the case there is always a strong suspicion of weak pasterns, a serious defect in the Bulldog.

Figure 4.

Figure 4. The perfect foot; a sound compact formation, with the desired very slight outward turn. The toes are well split up, but without much space between. The knuckles are prominent and high. The foot is of medium size, moderately round, with large pads. A dog with this formation is active on his feet, and not easily lamed.

THE TAIL

A serious fault in the present-day Bulldog is the high set-on and badly carried tail. As this fault is an increasing rather than a diminishing quality, it seems as if the time had arrived when the breeder will be compelled to give this matter his more serious attention. Probably in no other breed has the tail-carriage so much effect on the general appearance of the animal as it has in the case of the Bulldog. A tail low set-on, with unobtrusive carriage, has a powerful effect in giving the necessary "finish" to the dog. On the other hand, there is no more serious blemish on an otherwise fine specimen than the high set-on, "gaily" carried tail. Though in many other breeds this may be a very desirable "point," it is thoroughly out of harmony with the general lines of the Bulldog, and even tends to make him look ridiculous.

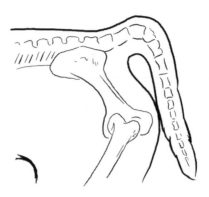

Figure 1.

Figure 1. This is the high set-on and coarse tail, which is invariably accompanied by a straight back, and is a very bad fault, even should the dog be trained or cowed to keep it down on special occasions.

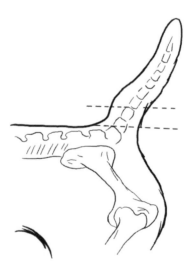

Figure 2.

Figure 2. This is the high set-on, coarse and "gaily" carried tail, which effectually tends to destroy all Bulldog character.

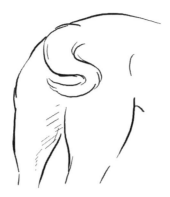

Figure 3.

Figure 3. This is a *malformation*, and is known as the "kink" or "screw" tail. This formation is, unfortunately, very prevalent at the present time. Indeed, there are still to be found "fanciers" who are under the belief that this is the correct form of tail. Though this tail does not detract from the general appearance of the dog to the same extent as shown in Figs. 1 and 2, it is certainly a most offensive form.

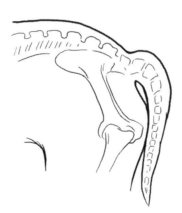

Figure 4.

Figure 4. This is the perfect tail, correct to standard requirements, low set-on, nicely tapering to the point, and carrying out harmoniously the graceful sweep of the hock.

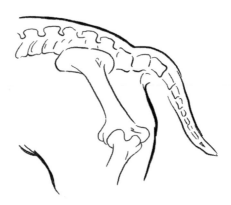

Figure 5.

Figure 5 shows the carriage of the perfect tail when the dog is on the alert or excited. Even under these conditions there is nothing obtrusive about the carriage: it will be observed from Figs. 4 and 5 that though the set-on to the spine is decidedly firm there is not the slightest tendency towards "gay" carriage.

C H A P T E R

4

The Value of the Pedigree

An accurate pedigree tells you, as far back as you are willing to research, the complete lineage of your dog, providing a host of clues to its genetic heritage. However, unless you have a thorough knowledge of the attributes and faults of the dogs in the pedigree, that impressive-looking document is just a meaningless list of names on another piece of paper.

There have been many top-winning, historically significant champion dogs and bitches who have consistently produced mediocre offspring. There have been others who, although they may have produced an occasional quality specimen that may have attained some measure of renown, were nonetheless more distinguished for throwing one or more of the following blemishes: blue eyes, pinched nostrils, high tail sets, palate problems, narrow fronts, bad ear carriage, wry jaws, entropion, ectropion, weak hearts, camel backs, overly wrinkled heads, spina bifida, cross-paddling and severe hip displasia, among an unhappy assortment of other ills.

Fortunately for the Bulldog breed, there have always been those dogs and bitches who have produced high-quality stock regardless of which dogs they were bred to. If by design, or chance, dogs and bitches such as

Eng. Ch. Ocobo Slightly Noble, owned by Norman and Patricia Davis, was England's top-winning Bulldog, the breed leader in Great Britain in 1985.

these are bred to each other, then the offspring, if bred intelligently, are likely to become the foundation of the most successful families.

In any intelligently conducted breeding program, it is extremely important that one is aware of as much information as possible regarding the overall quality of the grandparents. Were those Bulldogs sound and did their conformation fit the breed Standard? Did the dogs whose names appear in the pedigree possess good temperament? Did the litters they produced reflect above-average overall quality, or did just an occasional quality specimen result? If the latter proves to be the case, then perhaps the choice of breeding partners should be reconsidered.

Serious breeders are less concerned with the number of champions that can be counted on the collective pedigree of two dogs to be mated

To the serious breeder, every new litter is a new beginning. These promising youngsters, bred by Bob and Lenora Kerr, represent hope for the future, a link with the past and the incentive to pursue a gratifying, if demanding, personal objective.

than they are about the quality and prepotency of the dogs themselves, and, of course, the quality of the offspring. Much of the "to-do" about the champion count in pedigrees generally is the result of the breeder being more concerned about the price that a puppy will bear when sold to a novice or first-time buyer, than in seriously trying to improve the Bulldog breed.

The abbreviation *Ch.* appearing in front of an individual dog's registered name does not necessarily mean that dog is an outstanding example of its breed. It simply indicates that any dog so titled met the requirements for earning its conformation championship. As with anything else, there are outstanding champions and average or even mediocre champions. The measure of any dog is the extent of its individual merit compared to the Standard and as a producer.

THE MODERN BRITISH GENE POOL

The British government imposes strict quarantine regulations on all dogs imported into the country. Any dog that enters the island must be quarantined for six months in a government-approved quarantine kennel before being allowed to enter the country. As a result, the entire dog population has become relatively static in terms of the ability to maintain a greatly divergent gene pool. The populated area of the United Kingdom is about half the size of the state of California with about twice the population. The end result of this circumstance is that breeders in the U.K. (principally England), are still working with the original gene pool nucleus that is the progenitor of the Bulldog as we know it today. In England, therefore, one does not see the enormous disparity of head shapes, etc., that we see in other parts of the world. Most of the established, respected breeders linebreed, but only to animals that meet the criteria described on page 64. Actually, they have little choice. However, a perusal of the dogs pictured in magazines will instantly identify the most successful breeders as the characteristics of their stock are set, those animals exhibiting a definable type. Granddaughters and grandsons of the "producers" are bred to each other, such that the offspring closely resemble their eminent forebears.

The two most prepotent Bulldog studs in Great Britain during the 1980s were not champions, but each in their turn routinely produced outstanding specimens and their litters were of better quality than would have been expected from the union, based on the conformation of the sire and dam. Those fortunate enough to acquire a dog and/or bitch from either of these stud dogs were off to a head start, provided that they bred their foundation stock judiciously.

TOO MUCH, TOO SOON

It is not uncommon that relative newcomers to the breed acquire an excellent bitch, and the owners, quite naturally, often return to the "mentors" from whom they bought the bitch, seeking advice for selecting the right stud dog or which dog they recommend. More often than not, the bitch is linebred to a stud dog from the mentors' stock, and the puppies produced are of good or satisfactory quality, and on occasion a champion may result from this kind of breeding. However, a problem that often arises is that now the novices may think that they are true breeders, because they have produced a champion. The new "experts" are now convinced

Ch. Kozabull Glynbourne Zeke (left), owned by Ed and Jean Kozatek and Claire Tomlinson, and his son, Ch. Satuit Windjammer, owned and bred by Betty Davey, pose with their owner-handlers for the photographer after sharing a winning day. Quality animals that produce quality in turn are one of the breeder's highest goals.—Sandy Tatham

that they know it all, when in fact all they have done is buy a good bitch from a good breeder, bred the bitch to the breeder's good stud dog, produced a champion from the sellers' hard-gained gene pool, and registered the litter with their new kennel prefix. The same bitch may be bred to another stud dog (hopefully two seasons later), and produce yet another champion. Often by this time, the new "breeders of champions" fail to listen to the advice of their former mentors, and embark upon a breeding program that, three generations later, bears little if any resemblance to the quality foundation stock with which they started. Some

Ch. TNT's Peanut Brittle, owned and handled by David Tackett, scores Best of Winners and Best of Opposite Sex under the author at the first Specialty show of the Lower Susquehanna Bulldog Club of Pennsylvania. The opinions of Specialty judges strongly impact breeders' future plans.—John Ashley

get discouraged and give up; others learn from the costly lessons that they gave themselves, and approach the breed with new vigor and common sense.

LINEBREEDING, INBREEDING OR OUTCROSSING?

When we stop to think about it, outcrossing is a very distant version of linebreeding. The modern Bulldog was bred from the few remaining dogs that were left after the breed fell into disrepute. Over time from this small gene pool, only the best were bred, making the available gene pool quite small.

No experienced breeder would expect to breed a short-legged bitch to a well-balanced dog and expect that all of the puppies produced would have the correct length of leg under them at maturity. Statistically, if there

Can. Ch. Hounslow Why Worry, owned by Charlie and Flo Kettle.

were four pups, one would favor the sire, one the dam, and the other two would be a combination of both. All four of the pups are now carrying the gene for short legs; therefore this must be borne in mind for when the time comes for them to be bred. If these puppies are sold to buyers who plan to breed without making the buyers aware of the genetic background of the dogs, then the potentially negative genetic inheritance of those dogs could be spread over a very wide area. Is this not an ethically questionable practice? Unless the bitch had some otherwise fantastic attributes, she should not be bred at all. If the breeder had a very strong conviction that this bitch would ultimately benefit the breed and desired to save a bitch from this union for him- or herself, then the only correct thing to do would be to spay or neuter the rest of the litter so as not to perpetuate breeding problems for others to cope with.

The breeder realizes, of course, that it will take about three or four generations of well-planned breedings in order that the short-legged gene is no longer dominant, but it will still appear on a fairly routine basis.

One approach to accomplishing the foregoing is to inbreed. A daughter of the short-legged bitch is bred back to the original well-balanced stud (her father), a bitch saved, then bred back again to her father. A bitch from this last litter can now be bred to a well-balanced grandson of the original stud, provided it is known from whence his entire gene pool is derived. There had better not be any short-legged dogs in the background, or the breeder may be back to the starting point. This works very well for breeders who know what they are doing. Inbreeding can also result in doubling up on background faults that others may have labored long in the vineyard of inheritance to weed out. The perfect dog (or breeder) is yet to be born, but it is the ongoing attempt to come as close as possible that constantly fuels the passion of the true breeder.

The last breeding mentioned in the previous paragraph could be described as linebreeding, that is, breeding to a relative that is not too close. An example of linebreeding would be grandfather to granddaughter,

Three of Lillian Davis's Terra Nova Bulldogs in a relaxed moment.

Ch. Happy's Brandy of Pedley, a Specialty winning bitch, owned by Ben and Barbara Hill.

uncle to niece, or cousin to cousin. However, as neither gene pool is dominant, greater care must be used in matching the breeding pair. Both sire and dam must be carefully considered, *fault* judged as compared to the Standard, and both must be well-balanced with no obvious defects. As the gene pool is not being doubled up, the results obtained are not as readily predictable. If both prospective sire and dam show a number of points that you are not happy with, some extra thought might be given to the wisdom of proceeding with the contemplated breeding.

Breeding a tall dog to a short dog does not produce a dog of medium height; it produces some tall and some short. Maybe—just maybe, a medium-sized dog *might* result, but this medium-sized dog will surely produce tall dogs and short dogs. It does not take a judge's eye to distinguish a tall dog from a short one; however, other Bulldog features are not as readily obvious.

THE CURSE OF KENNEL BLINDNESS

A few breeders tend to be "kennel blind"; they refuse to see the faults in dogs that they have bred. These people are doing the breed great harm (and nothing for their own reputation). Several dozen Bulldog puppies can, in a few years, produce several hundred Bulldogs that turn out to be those poor creatures that give the breed a bad name for poor health and temperament. Novice breeders would be well advised to seek the advice of more than one of the breeders in a given area who have reputations for knowledge and honesty before embarking on a breeding program. By so doing, many pitfalls can be avoided, both for the breed and the potential breeder.

The successful breeder has kept with it because his love of the breed is such that bad luck and unfortunate experiences cannot deter him—he knows that breeding fine dogs, like any other worthwhile goal, is not as easy as it appears to be at first glance. The successful breeder is part veterinarian, anatomist, psychologist and geneticist. The successful breeder has learned to understand pedigrees and to study and research the dogs named therein. The successful breeder also knows that the pedigree by itself does not make a dog good, bad or indifferent any more than any other family tree will.

CHAPTER

5

Stud Dogs—Resource at Large

THE AMERICAN KENNEL CLUB RECOGNIZES ANY REGISTERED MALE DOG OVER the age of seven months as a stud dog. The nomenclature "stud dog" is very loosely used. In reality, any dog that is capable of producing offspring could be so regarded. However, breeders of any dog breed, when proudly referring to their "studs" are, in fact, stating that they feel that their males exhibit strong, positive attributes that, when combined with those of a suitable, approved bitch, will benefit the breed in general, and the puppies produced from this union in particular.

Years ago the stud dog was considered by breeders to be very special, particularly in the manner in which he was housed and maintained. At that time, the school of thought was that a good stud dog, in order to be prepotent and have a strong libido, had to be kenneled in a different area from the bitches on the premises. Studs were fed raw meat as their diet along with a few other concoctions thought at the time to enhance the dogs' performance at stud. Needless to say, the stud dog of yore tended to be a little "on the wild side" when introduced to a strange person or a bitch in season, thereby giving the bitch owner the impression that the

Ch. Marinebull's All The Way, owned by Karl and Joyce Dingman and bred by Frank Cox, is to date the top sire in Bulldog history. Thanks to the use of frozen semen, his sons and daughters are still becoming champions long after his death.

dog was indeed anxious to do his work, when in fact the dog was only pleased to have some company. In the late 1960s and early 1970s some of the old-timers still adhered to these outdated practices.

Today's stud dog, by contrast, is just another member of the family, normally a perfect gentleman around the house, with bitches and with

Ch. Millcoat's Titus, owned and bred by Rod and Mel Berger.

visitors. He will often ignore a bitch (with whom he lives) in the earlier part of her season, not unduly pressing his attention on her until he is sure that the timing is right and that he has a willing partner. A "visiting bitch" is treated very differently. She is in strange surroundings, with strange people and a strange dog who, apart from his normal curiosity, knows that she is in season and understands why she has been introduced to him. Although the bitch is aware of her condition and teases the stud unmercifully, if the timing is not perfect (for her) and the stud makes advances, she is liable to snap at or even bite the stud, thereby making this, and possibly other mating experiences, unpalatable for the dog. Particularly with a young or virgin stud, any injury or attack by a reluctant bitch can have disastrous repercussions for the rest of the dog's life. The experienced stud dog will know the right time, and will usually manage his role without facing the fury of an indignant consort.

Few dogs of any breed are used at stud as compared to the total male population of that breed. In a week or two, a stud dog can sire more puppies than the average high-producing bitch can whelp in her lifetime. A sire's fame spreads fast when he is consistently doing "more than his share" by throwing his attributes evenly throughout his litters, producing an above-average number of get that are "show quality."

No stud dog can perform miracles in the whelping box. Breeding to a quality specimen that produces quality and that has been sensibly linebred can be a source of long-term benefits to a breeding program, provided that judicious use of pedigrees is employed with a true knowledge of the dogs and bitches whose names are contained therein. It is not unusual that three or more generations from the first breeding some dogs and bitches are produced that carry many of the attributes that were responsible for the original selection of the stud of choice.

Success as a stud dog and as a show dog are not mutually inclusive. Some Bulldogs that will walk well on a lead, are well behaved, and show themselves well in the backyard absolutely refuse to suffer the indignity of the showring. There is no point in trying to force these reluctant performers to show. To do so might only succeed in making them neurotic. There have been more than a few cases in which a particular dog is shown with great success, while his less formidable, less flashy, unknown litter brother stays at home enjoying the simple pleasures. One thing they do have in common is their pedigree. The stay-at-home dog can be a beautiful specimen and difficult to fault; both dogs share the same father and mother, they just don't share the grandeur and showmanship. However,

Ch. JC's Jon Boy Collins, owned by Jim and Corrine Winick.

Ch. Cherokee Yancey, bred, owned and handled by Cody Sickle, boasts a fine record of outstanding wins, including Best of Breed at the Bulldog Club of America 1985 Specialty under the esteemed breeder-judge Beryl Gould.—Roberts

in some cases, the relatively obscure *homeboy* proves to be a dramatically superior stud force than his illustrious brother.

HANDLING THE BULLDOG STUD

It has been said too often, and quite erroneously, that Bulldog studs cannot successfully consummate a mating without assistance, much in the same way that it is said that Bulldog bitches cannot free-whelp. It is true that Bulldogs are almost always bred with human intervention, but this is the choice of the breeders, not the dogs.

Ch. Bowag's Arthur de Day (Ch. Bowag's Airborne Sunny Day ex Ch. Hitchhiker de Bowag), owned and bred by Beverly and O'Neill Wagner, is a Specialty winner and the sire of twenty-six champions.—Stephen Klein

Ch. Aldridge Advent Gold, owned by Les Cotton, was the sire of England's first frozen semen Bulldog litter.

The reason behind such intervention comes from breeders, wanting to be certain that the correct dog is bred to the correct bitch. It is a way to be sure that all goes well in the course of mating. When matings are conducted during the summer months, extra care is necessary to avoid exposure for our Bulldogs and the chance of overheating. Very often the bitch owner insists on observing the proceedings, which can also add an unwelcome element of stress to the proceedings. With cooled and frozen semen being flown around the country, and indeed the world, the stud dog often is not even present at the breeding. The result is that the majority of breedings are accomplished by means of some form of artificial insemination.

To the newcomer, it may come as a complete surprise that many stud dog owners do not "handle" their own dogs at the matings. Usually there are a few stud dog handlers in any given locality who perform this service for the owners of the males. Many "studmasters" handle any given number of active males of a variety of different breeds with the same dispatch. Often an expert studmaster can make the difference between a successful mating and a frustrating failure.

Following the customary practice, the bitch is brought to wherever the stud dog is located. The stud dog is always expected to perform at his best, and the most suitable environment for the stud dog is in surroundings with which he is completely familiar and at ease. The bitch's function at this time is to be a receptacle for the stud dog's sperm. She must be handled gently and with consideration, but, as the timing is vital, the stud dog's ability to produce viable sperm is paramount.

To function as an effective stud, a dog's sperm count should be approximately 250 million, although some dogs have levels of over 350 million. The sperm count is particularly important when freezing a dog's sperm for future use. When the count is at higher levels, more straws (portions of semen) can be frozen, so that more bitches can be inseminated from a single ejaculate.

Among the tangle of myths thriving in the dog fancy, there is one that holds that the volume of semen produced by the stud dog is in direct proportion to his prepotency. Nothing could be farther from the truth. The semen that a stud dog delivers is composed of three distinct fractions. Assuming, as an example, that the total volume of

Ch. Bowag's Airborne Sunny Day, bred and owned by Beverly and O'Neill Wagner, is the sire of twenty-one champions, including Ch. Bowag's Arthur de Day, a noteworthy stud dog in his own right.

the complete ejaculate is 10 ccs, then the first half-cc contains material that acts as a bacterial cleanser of the bitch's vaginal tract. The second fraction, also about a half-cc, contains the actual sperm cells that will join with the bitch's eggs, forming *zygotes* that will ultimately become puppies. The third portion, 9 ccs (often called *backwash*), contains material that chemically "chases" the sperm to their ultimate destination.

The sperm can be checked under the microscope to determine viability. The "tadpole"-shaped cells must have long, perfect tails that are not stunted or split. The heads should have an aerodynamic shape and in this case, two heads are not better than one. The sperm should be extremely active, the tails wiggling furiously, and the great majority of the sperm moving in the same direction. No virgin dog that has not passed this simple test should be bred to any bitch; it is grossly unfair to the bitch's owner. The responsible stud dog owner has a duty to have the animal's sperm checked on a regular schedule.

Ch. Hetherbull Bounty's Frigate, owned by Jean and Robert Hetherington and bred by Roberta Arnold, established an impressive string of top wins in the early 1990s.

As stud dogs get to be about three years old, it is not uncommon that they develop mild prostate infections, such that the sizes of their litters are reduced due to the decrease in the motility of their sperm. In some cases, in dogs that had only been bred naturally and had too many consecutive breedings that proved unproductive, the sperm check disclosed that these dogs had ceased producing sperm altogether. A useful deterrent to mild prostate infections is the administration of 500 mg of Amoxicillin for five consecutive days each month.

FINDING THE BEST DAYS TO BREED

Often stud dog owners/handlers take the responsibility of ascertaining the optimum day(s) on which to inseminate the bitch, especially if the owner of the bitch has left her in their charge—which is a common occurrence. There are a number of options available to help determine the breeding day(s) most likely to result in pregnancy.

Ch. Kippax Fearnought, owned by Dr. John Saylor and bred in England by Harold Dooler, was one of the breed's most memorable standard-bearers. The sire of thirty-two champions, he remains only the second Bulldog in history to have won Best in Show at the venerable Westminster Kennel Club event.

Some bitches will stand for a dog from the onset, and for the total duration of their seasons. This willingness to accept the male from the first day of bleeding should not be taken as an indication of optimum timing. If the stud dog owner decides to breed, based on the bitch's receptive behavior, by the time that the bitch is clinically ready, the stud dog's sperm will be depleted, such that the chance of a pregnancy is doubtful. A stud dog's sperm is at optimum strength about ten days after the last ejaculation.

The most commonly used method of checking the bitch for breeding readiness is to take vaginal smears. This test, to be accurate, is only as good as the sample, and the smear test is often given a bad "rap" because the specimen is often contaminated. If the inside of the vaginal opening or the lips are touched by the swab used to gather the sample, there is a great risk of sampling blood and urine traces that have been present for days. Obviously presenting such a contaminated sample can only give questionable readings. Many bitches miss because of this type of sloppy sampling technique. When the test tells the sampler that the bitch is ready, it may already be too late.

A much better alternative is to use a *guarded* culture. A lubricated sterile tube of about three inches in length and one-half inch in diameter is inserted into the bitch's vagina, pointing upward toward her tail. The swab is slipped through the tube with about an inch remaining outside. After the sample has been collected, the swab is withdrawn, then *rolled* on a clean slide, stained with blue dye for about thirty seconds, washed with distilled water, allowed to dry, then observed under the microscope. When taking ovulation smears it is important that the bitch be checked at least every other day from the onset of bleeding until the sixth day, then every day thereafter. The smear test, however, is providing us with information that is about two days late. This is the reason we learn to breed bitches early, after taking vaginal smears on a regular basis so as to track the progress of the estrus cycle. The experienced breeder/smear tester often has as high as a 90 percent conception rate as a result of being able to pinpont optimum mating times. Remember, there is no guarantee that the bitch's season will be the same every time and there may be a significant variation in her estrus cycle the next time she is to be bred.

When shipping frozen or cooled semen, the smear test is of little value, as the two-day delay poses too much risk. Progesterone testing of the bitch's blood is the choice when shipping semen across considerable distances. This type of testing is more expensive, and until very recently, was not recommended for the lay dog breeder. The kits currently available also vary in cost and reliability. At one time veterinarians could come up with widely conflicting results from the same sample, as interpretation of the test was difficult. The test results are read in nanograms. The kits available read in the range of from three to eleven, with eleven being the optimum time to breed. Wider ranges of readings require sophisticated and expensive equipment that most veterinarians would not consider purchasing and serve little purpose in estimating the optimum time to breed. It is important, when purchasing a kit, that it is designed specifically for dogs. As with smears, interpretation of the test requires experience, and can vary with each individual. Suffice it to say that there are many in the breeding community who should leave the testing to their veterinarians.

As of this writing the top stud dogs in order of numbers of champions produced are:

Ch. Marinebull's All The Way	86
Ch. Millcoat's Titus	52
Ch. JC's Jon Boy Collins	50
Ch. Mim-Jim's Buckie Too of Cha-Ru	37
Ch. Hetherbull Bounty's Frigate	37
Ch. Kippax Fearnought	32
Ch. Cherokee Yancey	28

It is interesting to note that the great Eng. and Am. Ch. Kippax Fearnought was imported by Dr. John Saylor to Southern California in 1953, long before the use of frozen and cooled semen became widespread and the practice of shipping it across vast distances opened up a world of new possibilities for dog breeders. At that time it was not even practical to ship bitches! Ch. Kippax Fearnought was the second and, to date, the last Bulldog to win Best in Show at the Westminster KC. This happened in 1955, forty-two years after Ch. Strathtay Prince Albert scored the first Westminster BIS for the breed. One can't help but wonder what influence on the breed Fearnought could exert if he were alive today.

CHAPTER

6

The Role of the
Brood Bitch

THE TERM "BROOD BITCH" REFERS TO A FEMALE DOG THAT IS MAINTAINED FOR the sole purpose of producing offspring, and is an insult to any well-conformed bitch. Some years ago, a well-known, successful breeder, when proudly showing off her kennel and Bulldog stock, stated that some of the bitches she displayed were not good enough for showing, but that they were good enough to breed and would provide income to maintain the kennel and defray the expense of showing her better quality specimens. As much as we may look with disdain upon such an attitude, there are, unfortunately, people that operate by this kind of thinking in any pure-bred dog breed, and they don't belong in the fancy. Breeding inferior specimens can do nothing but harm to any breed. This is where many breeds get labeled with a bad name for questionable health and physical and temperament problems that are passed on to the unsuspecting buyer. If these buyers, in turn, breed in order to recover the "investment" in the purchased bitch, all the problems they got "stuck with" become that much more compounded.

Bunkie's Maybelline Shabrae, owned by Paula Broz, is a daughter of Ch. Jowtrix Barney Rubble and a successful brood bitch, having produced three champions in one litter.—Callea

The first-time buyer usually wants to buy a puppy at about eight weeks of age in order to form an early bond with the new addition. If the puppy was raised properly, then it has already bonded to the breeder. This is evidenced when the dog visits the breeder's home at about a year old, instantly recognizing the familiar surroundings and the breeder(s). They appear to be so happy that the new owner has hurt feelings. Fortunately, the Bulldog is happy with anyone that treats him or her well, and the new owners soon forget about the incident.

All Bulldog puppies at eight weeks of age look wonderful. They are playful, covered in wrinkles, and almost always appear to be short, little boxcars. However, many of these great looking puppies change dramatically between twelve and twenty weeks of age and turn out to be tall, long, gangly puppies that bear little relationship to the short, squat, potential champions they looked like in the nest. With such a bitch puppy, even if the pedigree is impressive, the probability that she will produce

Ch. LaBabe's Tina Maria Coqueta, bred and owned by Dave Williams.—Lindemaier

quality offspring is slim to none if she, herself, lacks any visible merit as an individual.

Before purchasing a Bulldog puppy of either sex, the buyer would be well advised to read the available literature, study the Standard and ask questions of respected Bulldoggers in the area, before even looking at a single litter. Then, armed with some understanding of the breed, the potential buyer can spend a couple of weekends looking at puppies. When first-time buyers follow this advice, they are always surprised that they quickly are able to recognize the difference in the quality of the various puppies in individual litters.

The best-case scenario in purchasing a bitch is to find a breeder who is willing to sell the aspiring novice a bitch that is eight or nine months old. At this age, her conformation is quite evident as she is suffficiently grown so that her positive attributes and faults (and she will have at least one or two) are readily discernible. In conjunction with a linebred pedigree, this balanced, sound bitch will take much of the guesswork out of breeding quality Bulldog puppies, provided she is bred intelligently. Needless to say, a bitch that one may use as a foundation for a serious breeding program will command a much higher price than an eight-week-old puppy. The extra money is well spent—her jaw, ears, tail set, front and rear movement, eyes, general health, temperament and a host of other attributes are easy to evaluate at this stage of her development. You really do get what you see. The very earliest writings on Bulldogs usually admonish the beginning breeder to always "buy the best bitch that you can afford."

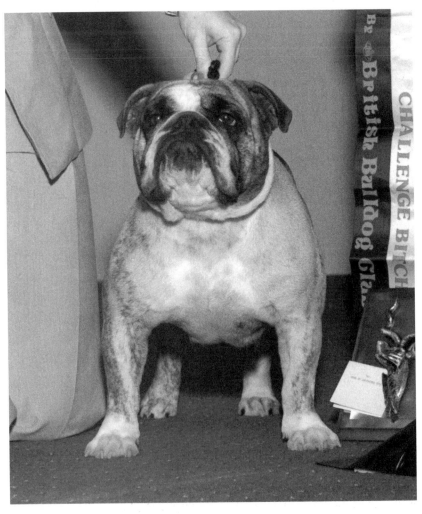

Ch. Chelsea's Sweet Dusty Rose, CD, owned by Pat Ropp.—Mikron

Ch. JK's Miss American Pie, a Best in Show winner, owned by Cathy and Jerry Pritchard.

In the wild, canine bitches, such as wolves, coyotes and foxes, among others, come into season only once a year. The wild dog has to forage for food, traveling long, hard distances in order to hunt smaller animals and seek out roots, berries, birds' eggs and all the other food sources that comprise their natural diet. It is a well-known fact that female athletes, particularly distance runners, temporarily cease to have menstrual periods, due in part to the burning up of protein. The domestic female dog is essentially spoon-fed, and if lucky, will get enough exercise to keep her fit. She will come into season, on the average, every six to eight months, but this does not mean that she should be bred at each season. Her body has not yet had time, in most cases, to recover from the effects on her body by the previous litter she whelped and raised. If her previous litter was delivered by cesarean section, her need for rest before being bred again is even greater.

In nature, a bitch whelps once, and only once, a year. Dogs are social creatures; they live in packs with a decided "pecking order." During severe winters, when there is insufficient food to properly feed the entire pack, nature makes the decision as to which bitch will or will not come into season, usually reserving this most crucial of responsibilities for the more mature, more experienced bitches that are able to fend for themselves and their offspring. The younger bitches, less mature in mind and body, are passed by, assuring survival of the species! Nature has a commonsense way of regulating the population growth of all wild species. It is sad that some breeders are not willing to adopt those proven principles of nature that apply even in our artificial environment.

The bitch to be bred should meet the criteria that will render her suitable to her important purpose, healthy in mind and body, possessing attributes that will benefit the breed, exhibiting balance so that no one feature stands out in comparison to any or all others. Likewise, the stud dog chosen should be a good match—strong in the bitch's excellencies as well as in her shortcomings. Arrangements should have been made well in advance so that the stud dog has been reserved, the appropriate fees have been agreed upon and the means of safely transporting the bitch to the stud have been set.

Most bitches give advance warning that they are about to come into season. Upon observation, the vulva will become noticeably "puffy" from one to three weeks before the onset of bleeding. In rare cases, a bitch may

Merriveen Jasmine, shown at ten years old.

Eng. Ch. Bullzaye Phyllis Dixie, owned by the late Richard and Betty Cassidy. During the summer of 1986, Dixie lost her newborn litter as a consequence of unusually hot local weather. Two days later, her litter sister died whelping her litter, but Dixie successfully raised her orphaned nephews and nieces.

have a *silent season* in which bleeding does not take place, although the puffiness is evident. The alert breeder will conduct the necessary tests, which are described later, to determine whether or not the bitch is actually in season and proceed accordingly. If the timing is correct, the breeding in silent season has as good a chance of being as successful as with a normal season.

The very earliest that a bitch should be bred is on her third season; her age will range from eighteen months to two years or more. By this time she should be mature in mind and body, although some bitches will not conceive before they are three years old. It does seem that the biology governing the breeding of Bulldogs never follows the normal patterns that apply to other breeds.

In the scientifically aware world of modern dog breeding, certain conditions must be guarded against before any mating is consummated. A particularly important disorder to protect breeding stock from is canine infectious brucellosis. This is a virulent form of canine venereal disease for which your bitch should be checked by your veterinarian long before breeding, and treated if necessary. A diseased dog or bitch will not be able to produce puppies, and can easily infect a clean partner. Today, wise stud dog owners and handlers require proof of brucellosis testing before a breeding is approved.

Before dog breeders had the now-commonplace capacity to use ovulation smears and luteinizing hormone testing, the standard practice was to breed the bitch on about her ninth and eleventh days of *color*. Timing for optimum chance at conception was once a pretty hit-or-miss affair. Some veteran breeders considered that the most reliable test was to insert a covered finger into the bitch's vulva and hope that her internal genitalia would clamp down on the finger. If this happened, it was considered a reliable indication that she was now ready to breed and at an optimum point in her cycle for conception to occur.

Few breeders used the services of veterinarians for collecting and reading ovulation smears—with good cause. A large number of veterinarians lack sufficient experience in this area and often collect specimens and read smears incorrectly. Going back to previous remarks about the use of the guarded culture, if a speculum is not first inserted into the bitch's vaginal opening, the long swab will first come into contact with dried blood that may have been discharged days earlier, thereby giving a

Ch. Li'l "00" Trouble, with her nine-week-old puppies, Graybull's Lord Fawnallover and Graybull's Abba-Zabba, owned by Bill and Kay Gray.—Jerry Vavra

completely inacccurate reading of the smear being taken. By definition, a speculum is a hollow, fairly narrow diameter tube, such as a hypodermic syringe cover, through which the swab is inserted. The syringe cover is about three inches long, allowing the swab to pass protected through the area of occult blood without contamination, assuring a clean, fresh, reliable sample.

The use of ovulation smears serves another very valuable purpose; if the bitch has a bladder infection, it will be readily apparent to the trained eye, enabling the bitch to be cleared up of any minor problem before a breeding is actually undertaken. As Bulldogs are normally very low-slung, and as bitches in season are even closer to the ground when urinating, it is fairly common for them to contract low-grade bladder infections by this mechanical means. Until the advent of Baytril a few years ago, it was a common practice to administer antibiotics such as Amoxicillin in 500-mg doses per day until the end of the breeding period. Now, however, it is a common practice to administer Baytril No. 60 on the first

Not all show dogs strive for conformation championships or obedience titles. This is "Daisy Buchanan," who doesn't do dog shows but is a natural in commercials, and is the special joy of owner Susan Luck Hooks.

day of color for about six or seven days, with the certainty that any minor infection will be eliminated by the end of the course of treatment.

It was previously observed that an "average" time to breed a bitch is roughly from her ninth to eleventh days, but, as with all things Bulldog, this is true only some of the time. In actual fact, each bitch can be different from one season to the next, and may well have an optimum day on which to breed, at five days from color in one season to as much as thirty-plus days from color on another season. A bitch may come into season for a week, go out for two or three days, and come back in season again, at which time she is breedable.

Many bitches have a false season on the fourth month after whelping. They have a bloody discharge that lasts for only a few days, then recycle normally again at about six months or more from the whelping date. Similarly, false pregnancies can occur. Whether the bitch was bred or not, the bitch exhibits the same symptoms as in a normal pregnancy, such as swollen teats, nesting, digging, etc., but in their mind they whelp a couple of weeks earlier than in a normal pregnancy and adopt an inanimate object such as a toy as their whelp, caring for it as if it was a real puppy. Fortunately this only lasts for two or three weeks before they return to normal.

Ultrasound testing to determine pregnancy has recently become so inexpensive that much of the worry and guesswork as to whether the bitch is actually in whelp can be completely avoided. The test procedure is quick, simple and totally harmless to the bitch and her puppies. The optimum time to perform the test is about four weeks from the breeding date. It is important to allow the bitch to drink plenty of water before going for the test, and equally important that she is not allowed to urinate until after the test is completed. The water in her system helps amplify the sonar bounce, making the images of the fetuses more readable.

CHAPTER

7

Contracts

WHENEVER PUPPIES ARE BOUGHT AND SOLD, WHENEVER A STUD DOG SERVICES a bitch, considerable discussion ordinarily takes place between the parties involved. Unfortunately, we all don't remember the same things in the same way with the passage of time, and relationships can become unnecessarily strained between the involved parties as a result of a difference of opinion, however minor. Therefore, with any transaction involving valuable animals, it is foolish not to commit the entire agreement to writing, signed by both parties with each retaining a copy. The agreement should be discussed in advance of the service being provided, and the "contract" read and signed before breeding your bitch, using your stud dog, or a puppy is bought or sold.

Today's purebred companion dogs can probably be classified as luxury possessions. The Bulldog in particular is routinely a very expensive, man-made breed. Semen or bitches are shipped across the country, costly blood tests are conducted, and high veterinary costs are often incurred in the normal collection and insemination process. Cesarean sections are routinely performed on Bulldogs. The end result is that an eight-week-old pet-quality puppy purchased from a reliable breeder, dependent on the

Ch. Bullzaye Sandy McNab at fifteen months, owned by Richard and Betty Cassidy of Lancashire, England.

population density, can cost from $800 to $1,200, or more. Current AKC registration statistics indicate that the average litter of Bulldogs registered consists of about three puppies. However, most litters at birth contain a much higher average that decreases due to the mortality rate, contributing to the additional cost of the surviving puppies available for sale.

The examples that follow have proved to be very useful, and may be adjusted according to individual needs. Although every effort is made to ensure that a puppy is going to a good home, occasionally the buyers turn out to be different from what they first appear to be. They may dote on the dog, but can be forever demanding of the breeder.

A breeder cannot be held responsible if a puppy was bitten by a spider a month after the purchase, causing temporary inflammation or

Mrs. White King Rock at six months, owned by Cary and Roz Appel.—Ashbey

99

lameness. The breeder should not be required to pay any resultant veterinary expenses, or be the subject of a lawsuit.

YOUR LOGO, KENNEL NAME, ADDRESS, PHONE, FAX

SALES AGREEMENT

This sales agreement applies to an AKC registered Bulldog, or to an AKC registered Bulldog litter.

The litter number or individual registration number is:
Sire:
Dam:
Sex: Color:
Date of Birth:

Seller(s) certifies that the above described Bulldog is of sound health at the time of this sale. Buyer(s) is advised to have this Bulldog examined by a competent veterinarian of his/her choice (preferably with experience in the breed, e.g., Dr. Peter Wonderful, Hollywood, CA) within forty-eight (48) hours from the time that delivery of this dog is taken. Buyer(s), if so recommended by their veterinarian, may return this dog for full refund or credit towards another dog. Buyer(s) MUST provide the veterinarian's opinion in WRITING in the event of a return.

Seller(s) are NOT responsible for the health of this dog after the forty-eight (48)-hour period. Seller(s) cannot guarantee that a male puppy will have two normally descended testicles at maturity. Seller(s) cannot guarantee the fertility of a puppy at maturity.

In the case of an unconsummated sale, deposits remain with the seller(s).

Buyer(s) understand that a normal Bulldog can have medical anomalies that are not common to other breeds, as a result of breeding genetic defects to produce the unique dog that we have today. The medical treatment of the Bulldog requires specialized veterinary knowledge and experience.

The sales price of this Bulldog is $:
Additional Conditions:
Seller's Signature:
Print Buyer's Name:
Buyer's Signature:
Buyer's Address:
Buyer's Telephone:
Date:
Dr. Peter Wonderful (123) 456-7879

BUYERS UNDERSTAND THAT, IF FOR ANY REASON, AT ANY TIME THE BUYER IS UNABLE TO KEEP THIS DOG, THAT THE DOG WILL BE RETURNED TO THE SELLER.

In the state of California the following document is a required part of the sale of a dog in addition to any other documents that may be required. As of this writing I am uncertain as to whether or not it is required in other states.

DOG PEDIGREE REGISTRATION DISCLOSURE

Description of dog:
The dog you are purchasing is registered/registerable (circle one) with the American Kennel Club, United Kennel Club, States Kennel Club, Other (circle one).

Registration means only that [enter name of registry] maintains information regarding the parentage and identity of this dog. It does not guarantee the quality or health of this dog, and it does not guarantee quality lineage. Since dog pedigree registries depend in large part on the honesty and accuracy of persons registering dogs, registration does not guarantee the accuracy of the lineage recorded nor that this dog is purebred.

Acknowledged Date:

Ch. Arthurian's Spartacus Spike, owned and bred by Arthur and Phyllis Palacious is a multiple Specialty winner.

RDOGS FORM 1/92

When a visiting bitch has been bred to your stud dog, the following form is useful in keeping the bitch's owner apprised of the do's and don'ts regarding the maintainance of their bitch during the gestation period:

YOUR KENNEL NAME
ADDRESS, LOGO

Your bitch named "Whatever" AKC # 12345678/01 was bred on _____ and her whelping due date is approximately _____.

Please take note of the following "do's" and "don'ts":

Do not flea dip your bitch as harm can be done to the puppies.

Immediately give the bitch 800 micrograms of folic acid daily (available in tablet form from any health food store).

Do not administer excess calcium (except calcium gluconate) to the bitch until she is in her eighth week of pregnancy. Normal vitamin pills are OK.

In the last three weeks of her pregnancy, feed twice a day; split the normal amount of food in half for each feeding. Feed **recommended brand** mix by **manufacturer of choice.** In the last week of pregnancy (after a bowel movement), take her temperature two or three times a day to establish her "baseline" temperature. All dogs' "normal" temperatures are not necessarily 101.6 degrees; many Bulldogs' "normal" can be 100.5 degrees. Her temperature may drop as low as 98.0 degrees when she is due to whelp, but this is not always the case, so you must use your personal knowledge of the bitch and look for signs of contractions, i.e., a ripple along her sides. If she is carrying a large litter, none of the foregoing may occur.

Call if you need advice. The stud dog used was CH. ABCDEFGHIJKL AKC # 12345678/01.

Ch. Graybull's Alpine White Lace, bred and owned by Bill and Kay Gray.—Mitchell

We recommend Dr. Wonderful, Tel. (123) 456-7879, a fine veterinarian who is highly experienced with the special needs and problems of the Bulldog breed.

STUD SERVICE CONTRACT

YOUR KENNEL NAME, LOGO, ADDRESS, PHONE, FAX

This is to certify that:

The Bulldog Bitch_____ AKC#_____

Owned By_____ Address_____

Was Bred to My Stud Dog_____ AKC#_____

Date Bred:_____Whelping Due Date(s):_____

Cash Fee: $_____

Additional Conditions:_____

CONDITIONS OF SERVICE AS PART OF THIS CONTRACT

No fee refunded in whole or in part. Only a guarantee of actual breeding is made, not of pregnancy or of puppies living or dead. If the bitch fails to be in whelp (pregnant), the owner must give notice to me not later than fifty-five (55) days after the date of the last breeding. A RETURN SERVICE will be given by the same stud WITHOUT CHARGE at the next heat (and only that heat). Unless such notice is given, the right of a return service is forfeited.

If my stud dies, is sold, or is otherwise not available, I have the right to breed the bitch to another stud of my choice, unless mutually agreed between both parties on another stud. If the ownership of the bitch changes, right of return service is at my option.

Ch. Isgraig Black, owned by Roz and Cary Appel.—Ashbey

In order to assure myself of the pregnancy of the bitch, the right to see and examine her is hereby granted.

If a puppy(ies) is (are) to be received instead of a cash fee, I will make my final choice(s) of litter at eight (8) weeks of age. *However*, the right to examine the puppies within eight (8) hours of birth is hereby granted. One puppy constitutes a litter, and if there is only one puppy, regardless of sex, this puppy shall constitute my choice of litter. *At my option*, the bitch owner may buy the single puppy from me at the cost of a puppy as advertised in the local newspapers less the stud fee paid. If all puppies are born dead, or none survive to the age of eight (8) weeks, I have the postponed right to choice of a puppy through mating to my stud at the heat following the next heat, *but* a repeat service is at my option. *No cash* compensation is due me in this event. If the same

Ch. JB Rare Amazing Grace, a Best in Specialty winner, bred by John and Susan McGibbon and co-owned by them with Warren and Linda Thornton.—Missy Yuhl

condition occurs at the second whelping, obligations of both parties to this contract are terminated. These rights (choice of puppy[ies]) are not affected by change of ownership of the bitch. The bitch owner hereby agrees to inform any new owner of this contract.

By this contract it is specifically agreed that the stud dog owner is not obligated to sign the application for registration of this litter, until, and unless, the stud fee has been paid in full, or, in the case of a puppy(ies) fee, the stud dog owner has taken possession of the puppy or puppies as agreed.

Signed Stud Owner(s)_____
Signed Bitch Owner(s)_____
Date:_____

CHAPTER

8

Raising Bulldog Puppies

THE BITCH TO BE BRED MUST BE IN GOOD GENERAL HEALTH, FREE FROM PARA-sites, and in trim condition—carrying neither too much nor too little weight at the time she is bred. As noted in previous chapters, the effort is for naught if she is bred to anything less than the best genetically compatible stud dog available.

Feed the future mother a top-quality puppy food throughout the gestation period. In my opinion supplements are not necessary although some people do like to use them. Give the bitch 800 micrograms of folic acid (B-complex vitamins) daily in pill or capsule form with her food (or wrapped in her favorite treat). The folic acid is useful in eliminating or reducing the instance of cleft palates and *Anasarca* (water) puppies. Start administering the folic acid when the bitch is being bred. Avoid at all costs giving the bitch excess calcium (except for powdered calcium gluconate) until the eighth week of pregnancy, as the bitch's body eliminates calcium that it does not need.

The puppies' growing skeletons are composed of calcium, and if the bitch does not get enough of this important mineral during gestation, the unborn puppies can therefore be severely damaged from the lack of

Ch. Jowtrix Barney Rubble, owned by John and Susan McGibbon, has established himself as a successful sire of winning offspring.

Ch. Hug-O-Bull's Redskin Rhumba, a multiple Specialty show and Non-Sporting Group winner, bred and owned by Frank, Norma and Elizabeth Hugo.

calcium and other necessary minerals. If you are certain of the bitch's due date, calcium must be administered five to six days before her whelping date. A dosage of 250 milligrams daily is sufficient; however, if your bitch was mated several times and you have several due dates, it is preferable to wait—better safe than sorry.

From the time the bitch is bred, do not use any flea spray or flea dip on her of any kind. Doing so can have a disastrous effect on the puppies; those that do survive will not come up to your expectations in any way. If you discover fleas on your pregnant bitch, patience, a flea comb and rubbing alcohol should get the job done.

Sixty-three days is generally assumed to be the gestation period for Bulldog bitches, just as for bitches of any other breed. However, when only one unaided natural breeding has occurred, we have never known of a bitch that has gone past sixty-one days.

You will need certain supplies for the approaching whelping, so while you are waiting for your puppies to develop, the following materials should be on hand in anticipation of the big day:

Rectal digital thermometer

Lubricant

Small heating pad or hot-water bottle

Cardboard box twice the size of the heating pad

Terrycloth towels

Infant nasal syringe

Four-ounce baby bottles fitted with Gerber orthodontic nipples

Liquid or powder bitch's milk replacer

Nemex wormer

3-cc and 10-cc syringes (without needles)

Ten-pound scale

Playskool baby soft food bottle

Gerber first food baby rice and Gerber first food baby lamb

Small heating light bulb on a clamp

Two child's wading pools eight inches deep by three feet in diameter (or build your own whelping box)

Exercise pen measuring four feet square by about two and a half feet high

Using the thermometer, take the dam's rectal temperature on a consistent basis during her eighth week of pregnancy. Digital thermometers do away with much of the guesswork of taking temperatures—they beep when the maximum temperature has been reached. The normal temperature for a dog is 101.5 degrees F. Bulldogs, however, tend not to conform to many of the givens that normally apply to other breeds, so take her temperature two or three times a day, starting a week before her first due date, preferably after a bowel movement, as her temperature will read lower than the actual if you do not take this precaution. It is not uncommon that a Bulldog bitch's ambient temperature a week before she reaches full term measures only 100.5 degrees F. The prospective dam will also have to urinate much more frequently than normal, so be sure to let her out for this purpose according to her regular schedule and for any other "pit stops" she signals she wants. Remember, the dam is eliminating for the puppies as well as for herself, so if the bitch doesn't—they don't. This is vital to the "puppies" and their dam's well-being.

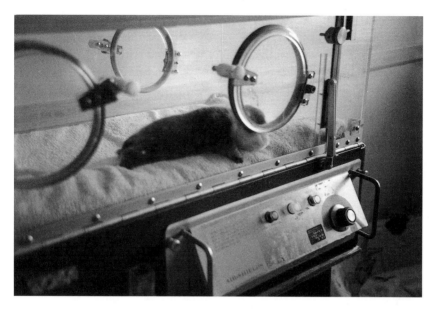

When the need arises, the baby "isolette" is a useful piece of equipment for getting Bulldog pup-pies through their first critical days.

In her last week of pregnancy, the dam will be very uncomfortable and will be experimenting with various parts of the house in order to find the right spot to have her family. This is the perfect time to introduce her to the whelping area you have provided. The reason that the two wading pools are often preferred over heavier, more cumbersome wooden whelping boxes is that they are inexpensive—especially at the end of summer, and when one is in use the other can be soaking in bleach wa-ter, they can be rinsed out with a garden hose, then wiped dry in a very short time. They are very light, easy to store, and big enough for the av-erage size Bulldog bitch with a litter of six or eight puppies. It is a good idea to alternate the pools every other day, to keep the puppies' environ-ment as clean as possible. To introduce the expectant mother to the wading pool whelping box, place inside the pool a few items with which she is familiar and attached to, such as her favorite blankets and toys. Most breeders raise their puppies in an area adjacent to the kitchen, if not in the kitchen itself, depending on the available space. When it be-comes necessary many breeders will not hesitate to shove the kitchen table aside in order to make room for the whelping quarters and to allow the bitch to feel unfettered and at ease. Feed the bitch in her whelping area,

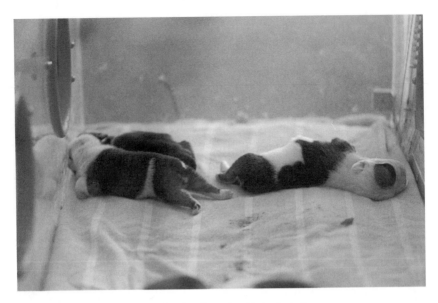

These week-old puppies appear relaxed and comfortable in the isolette.

making sure that this is where her water is at all times. She will soon accustom herself to sleeping and resting in the area where she will soon be whelping. When her time is coming near, she will dig and rearrange the blankets and towels in her pool. She will also grasp the blankets with her teeth and try to shred them as she holds them down with her paws. This is all in preparation for the whelping process, and is quite normal. As previously stated, if the bitch is so distended with puppies that her sides are tight and her underbelly is unyielding to gentle squeezing pressure there is a possibility that her temperature will not drop to the desired 98 degrees, at which point you would be safe to assume that puppies could be expected within the next two to six hours.

If the bitch has been refusing food and water for the past twelve to sixteen hours and she is breathing with a rasping sound (instantly recognizable even to the inexperienced) and if the day is consistent with her due date(s), and you know your bitch well enough to be sure that she is letting you know that she is ready, then you must face another decision.

Many young Bulldog bitches, about eighteen months of age, have free-whelped, *i.e.*, had their puppies naturally. However, in most free-whelped Bulldog litters at least one puppy is usually lost in the process. The wisest course is to take the bitch to your veterinarian when you think that she is finished having her puppies in order to positively ascertain that she has indeed completed the process. She will require an examination, possibly an X ray, and will be administered antibiotics as required. The puppies should also be checked at the same time. If the birth occurs, as births often do, when your vet does not have hours, then your only option is to take the whole family to the local emergency clinic. This will probably be considerably more expensive than normal charges for similar services. Of equal or even greater concern, you will almost surely be faced by a veterinarian with little or no knowledge of the peculiarities of the Bulldog breed. This all sounds terrible and it often can be but it happens with high frequency under the foregoing circumstances. Your long-awaited first litter can become a very expensive, harrowing experience, not to mention the potential of unnecessarily losing puppies, one of which may have had the opportunity to be of value to the breed—who knows? Many experienced breeders who have been through this experience when they were starting out would not attempt a free-whelping today. Almost without exception Bulldog breeders today choose to have their litters delivered by cesarean section. However, the ultimate decision to this question for your bitch must be yours to make!

Whether you decide to go "natural" or by section, your veterinarian should have been made aware of, and have examined your bitch to evaluate her condition. Assuming that a cesarean section is *planned,* and also assuming that the bitch is having a fairly routine pregnancy, then the following scenario should occur.

Your bitch has been unsettled for about a day and a half, tends to be very uncomfortable, and looks for something to rest her head on in order to be able to breathe with less effort. She may go to a corner of the room and let the walls hold her head for a while. She will come to you and stare, seeming to ask, "Why did you get me in this condition?" She doesn't seem to want to eat, and her breathing is now coming in a deep rasping sound. She is ignoring her water dish. Her temperature has been fluctuating between mid-99 to mid-100 degrees for the last two days and her large belly is no longer carried under her ribs, but has moved more to the rear and is now closer to her rear legs, making it difficult for her to walk. When the rasping begins, her temperature will now be taken on a more frequent schedule, i.e., every hour or so. You watch the clock, making sure that you will have enough time to get to the vet. Out comes the

Wencar Silver Drop with her five-day-old litter.

calendar and the breeding dates are checked for the fiftieth time, even though you know them as well as you do your own name! The temperature reads 98.8 degrees—you check the clock—still four hours until the vet closes—you wait a few minutes, then call your vet—your vet suggests that you take her temperature again—99.5—now what to do? You go back to the calendar—from the last breeding the youngest that the puppies could be is . . . ? What did my bitch's breeder tell me? At fifty-six or fifty-seven days the puppies will stand a very poor chance of survival. At fifty-eight days their chances are better, and at fifty-nine or sixty days it is pretty safe for them to make their appearance. You check the temperature again—99 degrees Fahrenheit on the button. The puppies must be at least fifty-nine days in the womb by this time. Zero hour has arrived!

When you get to your veterinarian, your bitch will have her temperature read again. The doctor will determine whether the bitch is dilated and question you about the breeding dates to be certain that you are sure. Even the most experienced breeders can get nervous when it is their own bitch that is involved. However, it is still *your* responsibility to make the final decision on whether or nor to go ahead with the surgery.

116

A four-week-old threesome with JB Rare Moses in the middle.

From the time that the decision is made to perform the cesarean section until the bitch has her incision closed, approximately one hour will have elapsed. As the doctor is closing, assistants will be attending to the umbilical cords. In natural births, the dam cuts the umbilical cords and leaves them about one inch long. She does so by pinching and flattening the cord where it is attached to the puppy. She does this several times along the length of the cord until she has decided upon the ultimate length. The result is that the cord appears to be spiraled, and flattened in several places.

A naturally removed umbilical cord stays on the puppy for several days longer than if it was surgically cut and tied. Perhaps veterinarians should give this some thought! It is not uncommon that Bulldog puppies exhibit umbilical hernias for the first several months of their lives. Happily, in almost all cases the condition corrects itself by the age of eight or nine months. Many uninitiated veterinarians, and some textbooks, declare that this is a genetic defect; it is not.

Many breeders have had problems with first-time buyers who have insisted on going to the vet that they have taken their other pets to for

These inquisitive six-week-old puppies are by Ch. Merriveen Windy Daze out of Ma Barke of Killarney.

years, and with whom they understandably feel comfortable. However, when they are told that the puppy has a genetic defect, they are distraught and call the breeder, who in turn advises them to go to Dr. Wonderful, who knows all about Bulldogs, and the problem is resolved—if the buyers listen. They don't always. Moral—have the buyers of your puppies go to a veterinarian that you know, and in whom you have faith. The same misdiagnosis often occurs with so-called heart murmurs in Bulldog puppies.

Just as you are more likely to encounter sick people in a hospital, sick dogs will normally be present at a veterinary clinic. When you take your bitch in for her "section," you certainly can't afford to have her come into accidental contact with any other dog present, and risk bringing home to her newborn puppies any diseases that she may pick up by walking on the clinic floor. It is therefore a good idea to wheel her into the surgery in a crate which has a top that opens. After the initial shots, which are easily administered to the bitch in the open-topped crate, she can be easily transferred to a holding pen until she is calm and has eliminated. At the conclusion of the procedure the new mother is transferred directly from the operating table to the open crate in which you have placed old towels, then wheeled to your vehicle and taken home without ever coming in contact with the clinic floor. Once home, she can rest in the crate until she decides to go "out."

At the beginning of the surgical procedure, plug in a heating pad and use it like a liner in the cardboard box that you have brought with you and placed adjacent to the operating table to receive the puppies. After the puppies are breathing normally, making all sorts of snuffles and grunts, and had their umbilical cords attended to, they can be taken home. The dam will usually sleep all the way home in the car, totally undisturbed by the crying puppies. If the puppies are not crying too much, then "rough them up" a little, as the crying lets more oxygen into their lungs and rids them more quickly of the anesthesia that they have ingested during the surgery. Roughing the puppies up simply means moving them about in the box. After a natural birth, the mother licks and rolls them around, such that you wonder why the puppies don't get damaged. When dealing with Bulldog puppies, always try to think of the wildlife programs showing canines that are presented on television. Puppies are not as fragile as they might appear on casual observation. If the dam decides to pick a puppy up in her mouth—don't panic. She knows what she is doing, so leave her alone.

After a C-section, the dam is somewhat confused from the combined effects of the anesthesia and the inevitable stress of any surgery. The speed and skill of the veterinarian has much to do with the recovery time of the bitch. The less time the bitch remains under anesthesia, the faster she recovers, and the greater are the puppies' chances of survival.

All newborn creatures have a little water in their system, mostly subcutaneously (under the skin), which is eliminated usually within twenty-four hours. The puppies have also been deriving in utero nourishment from their dam right up to the moment they were born. Therefore, it is not necessary to feed them immediately upon arriving home. Obtain in advance from your veterinarian liquid vitamin K-1, using a 1-ml syringe placed one-tenth of a milliliter under the tongue of each puppy as soon as you arrive home. This helps the puppy maintain viability during the first critical hours. Disturb the puppies frequently, as this will make them move around and encourage them to eliminate some of the water they were born with from their system. Allow the dam to rest until she is willing and able to feed her new family. You must also see to it that she goes outdoors frequently between her naps, and be sure to wipe her clean with a warm, moist towel and/or medicated wipes after each trip outside. After the dam leaves her crate for the first time, have her rest in her now-familiar whelping box, and change the towels in her crate immediately. When she reacts to the crying of the puppies, it is time for her to feed them. This response can occur at any time between two and four hours after arriving home, but each dam is different; some walk right in the front door when they come home, and demand their offspring immediately upon hearing them cry.

Hold the puppies to the dam's nose in order that she can smell them, then place the puppies between her front feet and encourage her to clean them while talking to the dam and stroking her gently. Some will set about to vigorously clean their puppies immediately, others often will have nothing to do with the puppies whatsoever and will turn their heads away. In extreme cases the dam may gag. Put all but one puppy back in the box with the heating pad, holding the remaining puppy behind the rear legs with the head facing towards your wrist, take hold of the dam's flew gently but firmly, and stroke the puppy's buttocks from the dam's nose to

"Somehow, I don't think these are Bulldogs." Six-week-olds are not too young to accurately size up a new situation.—Scherrer

120

Ch. L-N-N's Maximum Yardley Tucker, owned by Dr. Nancy Rose and Linda Tucker, as a puppy.

her mouth, causing the puppy to eliminate on the dam's face with the resultant licking to clean herself. It's extreme, to be sure, but it works! Go through this process with each puppy after first trying to encourage the dam to clean the puppy on her own. When all of the puppies have been cleaned, by whichever method, lay the dam on her side, and put the puppies on her nipples. With normal, healthy puppies, it shouldn't take long for them to react to their basic instinct to seek nourishment.

A new dam with a first litter may become very nervous during the feeding process, and can become startled at the slightest sound or movement. A sudden attempt on the dam's part to stand up or move in any way can be disastrous if she inadvertently rolls or stands on a puppy, so be by her side at all times during the feeding, especially for the first few days. A safe rule is—"do not leave the dam unattended when she is with the puppies." Most bitches pick up the routine after a few feedings and will accept their puppies willingly. In a very few days, when her maternal instincts and a strong flow of milk kicks in, the dam will demand her puppies on an ever increasing basis. The most important feedings are done in the first two days, as this is when the *colostrum* is available to the puppies from their mother. The colostrum provides "natural antibodies" contained in the mother's milk, and it is crucial that the puppies get this protection from their mother. It is their only means of immunity, as first shots are not generally administered until the puppies are between five and six weeks old.

Some breeders routinely keep a supply of frozen, colostrum-bearing goat's milk on hand in the event of emergencies. Obviously, this must be arranged for in advance, but goat's milk is not normally recommended. It contains little more than fat and its composition is suited to the needs of a very different kind of animal. Kids are able to stand, walk and run soon after birth and when they are born their eyes are wide open. Newborn kids also weigh about the same as a twelve-week-old Bulldog puppy. The breeder must rely on his or her own judgment on this point.

At the same time, if there are any other dogs in your household, keep them all as far from the newborns and their dam as possible. In particular, do not allow nonresident dogs to visit the house, nor the area in which the nursing mother is using as an exercise area. Many breeders insist that friends who visit take off their shoes at the door and spray their feet, ankles and hands with disinfectant before entering the premises. Responsible breeder visitors never ask to hold the puppies under any circumstances.

It normally takes two or three days for the dam's milk to increase to a volume sufficient to adequately feed four or five puppies. It is, therefore, quite customary to supplement normal, healthy Bulldog puppies with a quality bitch's milk replacement, using the Gerber orthodontic nipple. Barbara Hill, a successful Bulldog breeder of our acquaintance, has often been heard to remark that nursing dams should be equipped with gauges on their nipples. Be certain to heat the milk replacement to about 100 degrees. The milk from the dam is at her body temperature, so you, as the dog feeder, need to duplicate natural conditions as closely as possible.

Dependent on the size of the puppy, one-fourth to one-half ounce of fluid will be consumed after feeding on the dam. Remember, it is vital that the puppies eliminate before feeding. Until they are twenty-one days old, puppies do not have a gag reflex (they can't vomit), so they can ingest more food than they can handle and thereby get in trouble. If at any time during feeding, whether on the dam or from a bottle, milk is observed coming from the puppies' nostrils, immediately use the aspirator to clear the nasal passages. You can lose a puppy in a very short time from overeating. In all probability the puppy is too full, and this can trigger a perilous series of events. A too-full belly makes for difficult breathing, and if the nostrils are blocked the puppy can actually drown. All too many telephone calls have been received over the years describing this very circumstance that is readily avoidable by just paying attention to the minor details.

Few Bulldog litters are conceived by allowing the sire and dam to "tie" in the backyard. Most are the result of breeder-assisted natural matings, the use of artificial insemination involving fresh semen, shipped cooled semen, or breedings where bitches are shipped across the country and their litters are ultimately delivered by cesarean section. The Bulldog is totally the product of human intervention and it is not surprising, therefore, that the standard norms that apply to whelping in other breeds are routinely ignored by the Bulldog bitch. Do not leave the bitch alone with her puppies for even a second for the first few days. There are those who say that it is natural for the puppies to be with their mother, and that if any puppies die from the bitch's clumsiness that this was meant to be. Nature, however, does not use breeding boards, artificial insemination, cooled semen nor cesarean sections to produce new life. Nature is not lazy, and you must take a cue from this supreme teacher and give the puppies a chance. Stay with the dam until she understands and can handle the responsibilities that *you* have decided she must have.

SAFEKEEPING FOR BULLDOG PUPPIES

It often becomes necessary to keep Bulldog puppies in enclosures other than traditional whelping boxes. At these times puppies are maintained in a variety of containers, such as cardboard boxes, fish tanks, made-to-order wooden or plastic boxes, incubators and isolettes. The area should be large enough to hold the puppies until they are about two weeks old. A heating pad is placed at one end and the entire area is covered with a towel. The heating pad is set at low and left at that setting. The puppies will regulate their body temperature by crawling on and off the heated area as their need for comfort dictates. When changing the towels at each feeding, do not turn up the heating pad if the towel feels a little cold at first. So often puppies are lost because the heat is left turned up too high and forgotten, and the puppies become dehydrated as a result. If the towel feels too cold, put it in your microwave oven for about ten seconds. In the case of a box-type arrangement, drape a towel over the top of the box, leaving a gap of an inch or two at the end farthest away from the heat.

This will maintain the temperature in the box at about 82 to 85 degrees. When the bitch is not feeding the puppies, be certain that the box is in an area where she cannot get to it and accidentally pull it onto the floor.

FALSE PREGNANCY

Occasionally a bitch will experience a false pregnancy. While it can be a distressing nuisance to you, it is, however, very real to her. They go through all of the same symptoms as a bitch in whelp, such as nesting, shredding rugs, digging in the yard and so on. They usually go through their imagined whelping at about seven weeks from the time of breeding, if they would have been bred, and often adopt a toy or some other inanimate object that they keep by them and attempt to nurse for a few days, before giving up and returning to their normal routine. It is not unusual for spayed bitches to have false pregnancies also, and they often will have milk. A couple of my acquaintance own a spayed French Bulldog bitch that develops milk every time there is a newborn litter of Bulldog puppies in the household. She will take up residence in the kitchen near the whelping box, and becomes "mother's little helper."

When the puppies are first introduced to their mother for feeding, her milk should have been tested with "Nitrazine" tape, which is a form of litmus paper used for checking pH values between 4.5 to 7.5. The high range (7.0 to 7.5) is the reading that is necessary to the well-being of the puppies. It doesn't happen very often, but it is not uncommon that puppies have been lost due to the bitch's milk being "tainted" such that the puppies have green stools after nursing from their dam. Similarly, if the puppies cry a great deal after feeding, and upon examination their bellies have developed tiny, red, angry pimples, the chances are that they have contracted septicemia from their mother's system which is, of course, transmitted through the milk. If in doubt, bottle-feed until you can get the dam and her offspring to your veterinarian.

Before letting the mother have her puppies, make sure that she has been exercised, and that her nipples, incision and discharging vulva have been cleaned. As the dam is nursing she will normally breathe very heavily, especially after the first couple of days when her milk starts to come down. This heavier breathing is a good sign that the milk is coming down, and that her uterus is contracting.

124

At about ten days of age the puppies can usually be safely left in the care of their dam, as she will soon be giving serious thought to weaning the puppies anyway. At this age or within a few days, the eyes will be opening and the puppies will usually be standing, albeit unsteadily, as they prepare to commence with the subsequent phases of their lives.

WORMING YOUNG PUPPIES

Almost without exception, newborn puppies have some degree of worm infestation at birth. Even though the dam is presumably worm-free, she can harbor parasites in her system to which she carries immunity. The puppies, however, are not immune to these parasites (worms) which can be transmitted through the placenta before birth. Each puppy is accurately weighed and orally administered one-half ml (cc) per pound of body weight at two, three, four, six, eight and ten weeks of age. Many preventable puppy losses have been incurred as a result of worm infestation, so the wise breeder makes certain not to neglect this point. Happily, modern worming remedies are gentle to young puppies while effectively eliminating internal parasites. In such matters, be guided by your veterinarian, who can best identify the type of worm(s) you must deal with and the best drug to use against them.

WEANING

Often, when the dam is allowed to feed the puppies beyond twelve to fourteen days, she can become very uncomfortable, and can run the risk of developing impacted mammary glands, with an accompanying fever and the need for possible surgery. To avoid these possibilities, this is a good time to introduce the puppies to food other than their mother's milk.

Breeders who characteristically deal with large litters often give their puppies one or two tiny balls of raw hamburger meat at this stage. Now, when the dam attempts to clean her puppies, she becomes instantly aware that they have eaten something which did not come from her. This change of regimen greatly encourages the mother to wean the pups on her own, without being stressed by a sudden separation. At two weeks of age a commonly used puppy food mixture consists of one bottle of lamb

Eight-week-old puppies bred by Libby Moses, all "gift-wrapped" and ready to go to their new homes.

baby food, one cup of rice cereal and a half-and-half mixture of simulated bitch's milk and water blended or processed to a consistency of thin ketchup—too thick to go through the holes in the orthodontic nipple, but thin enough to be fed through the Playskool mush nipple.

At this stage the puppies are not in constant contact with their dam, they have the whelping pool all to themselves and have free access to a constant supply of fresh clean water, which they will immediately find and relish. The heating pad is placed under the bottom of the pool, in order that the puppies cannot chew on the electrical cord. This will become the puppies' sleeping area, with an exercise pen placed around the pool to contain the occupants, and a heat lamp clamped to the pen over the sleeping area, as the puppies are still too small to sustain body heat on their own as yet. Even in warm climates it can get too chilly for puppies at night.

Nails will probably have to be trimmed by this time, and inexpensive washable rubber-backed bathroom throw rugs with the rubber side up are helpful in giving the puppies the traction they need to learn to walk well. A small area is reserved for newspaper, which the puppies will soon learn to use as their toilet area. Make the carpeted area as bumpy as

"Are those bells ringing for me?"

possible by stuffing knotted old sheets or towels under the throw rugs—the rough uneven surface is an attempt to duplicate nature as closely as possible. Remember when the dam was digging a hole in the backyard? If she had had her way she would have had her puppies in the hole, and they would have had to stand up at a very early age. Experimentally it has been shown that puppies raised in this way had far superior hindquarters than those raised on a flat surface.

At three weeks the pups can digest well-soaked puppy meal mixed with rice cereal and the lamb baby food in a ratio of 60 percent puppy meal, 40 percent rice cereal, with a small bottle of the lamb. Introduce the pups to this new experience by feeding them the warmed mixture in a shallow dish placed on newspapers on the kitchen floor. Encourage them to lick the mush off of your finger and then from the dish. They will soon immerse themselves in the food and will need cleaning up with a warm, damp cloth after each meal. A day's supply, about four cups, can be made up at one time and refrigerated, then microwaved before feeding. The puppy food should be soaked in the refrigerator and well covered or the top layer will form a crust.

Toward the end of the third week, the rice cereal can be eliminated, and the soaked food microwaved, then mashed with a fork before

127

feeding. At four weeks the puppies will readily accept the puppy food without it being mashed. At this stage do not be surprised if the puppies appear to drink little water. They are getting plenty of moisture in the soaked food, but always have water with the pups anyway. Gradually, soak the food less and less until, by the fifth week, your little ones are on solid food, drinking water, and are becoming real little Bulldogs.

The puppies should be on puppy food for at least six months. Some of the less expensive puppy foods tend to give diarrhea to older puppies, so if premium food is not being fed, it helps to combine the puppy food with an adult formulation. Between the ages of six months and a year, adult food can be gradually mixed in until the puppy food is eliminated from the diet altogether.

INOCULATIONS

Puppy inoculations (injected vaccines) must be administered at six weeks of age. Generally, it serves no purpose to give the shots sooner, as the puppies are still using natural immunity and cannot assimilate the protection before this age. The standard five in one shots—"D.H.L.P.P."—contain the vaccines for Distemper, Hepatitis, Leptospirosis, Parainfluenza and Parvovirus. Some authorities suggest that the addition of Coronavirus vaccine is of little, if any, value. Bordtella vaccine, which safeguards against kennel cough and about two dozen respiratory diseases, is given at eight weeks of age, and can be administered nasally or by subcutaneous injection.

ASKING PRICES FOR BULLDOG PUPPIES

At the time this is being written and dependent on the area of the United States and the breeder's name and reputation, an eight-week-old puppy can sell for between $600 and $1,500. If the breeder also assures the buyer that the puppy is definitely of "championship" caliber, the asking price can be much higher. Generally, the younger the puppy, the riskier it is to make predictions regarding the individual. In Southern California the average price of a Bulldog puppy is $1,200. However, assuming that there are five puppies in the litter, and also assuming that the best puppies are sold first, is it fair that the buyer of the fifth puppy pays the same as the first? The answer to that poser is "yes," because if all the puppies received the same good care and all share the same good breeding, they should all have the same value. A given breeder is always free to attach any price he or she wishes to an individual puppy. Besides, if the first puppy is sold on the first of the month and the last goes ten days or two weeks later, it should have bearing on the price the breeder is asking or the amount the buyer is willing to spend. With fine dogs, as with anything else, you really do get what you pay for.

RAISING BULLDOG PUPPIES BY HAND

It may happen, for a variety of reasons, that a bitch is not able to successfully raise her own litter. Postpartum uterine infection, breast infection, toxic milk, eclampsia, an inadequate milk supply or even the death of the brood matron can bring about this unhappy situation. In such cases, puppies must be totally fed by hand, as opposed to the normal interventions of the breeder when the dam is healthy.

Bulldog puppies, whether hand-raised or not, should be weighed at birth as accurately as possible, using a gram scale. As there are twenty-eight grams in an ounce, a ten-ounce puppy will weigh about 280 grams. A one-kilogram scale (1,000 grams) can easily handle two-pound puppies. At this size your puppies should be on solid food and presumably out of danger. Beyond differences of weight and color, puppies must be marked in order to monitor their growth and keep an accurate record of weight and food intake. If necessary, experienced breeders use lengths of yarn or different colors tied around the neck of each puppy (and replaced as they grow) to tell them apart. The puppies are then referred to in your notebook as "blue boy," "pink girl," "green boy" or whatever. Of course, if you have a litter of four with a red dog, a brindle dog, a brindle bitch and a pied bitch, the yarn collars become academic.

ORPHAN PUPPIES

We never expect to lose our bitches during the whelping process, but it does occasionally happen, and most of us are not usually prepared for such a tragic turn of events. In this eventuality, one can attempt to obtain colostrum-bearing goat's milk, as mentioned earlier in this chapter, but it is not readily available in many places. It may be possible to locate a bitch of any breed who has whelped a litter in the past twenty-four hours and could give orphan puppies some immunity through her colostrum. If you find yourself in this situation, ask your local veterinarian if such a bitch is available. Most breeders are happy to help out if at all possible. If colostrum is not available, the litter will be totally without immunity until age six weeks, when first shots can be given. These puppies' lives depend on the breeder's ability to provide a properly hygienic environment in which they may grow. Puppies that have not received colostrum soon after birth are highly susceptible to a variety of dangerous diseases, as they lack passive immunity.

Orphan puppies are weighed at birth and then at four-hour intervals around the clock for the first four days and at eight-hour intervals thereafter, until they reach age two weeks. All feeding equipment must be thoroughly scrubbed and sterilized in boiling water after each feeding. No visitors should be permitted in the same room with orphaned puppies. Many diseases, including distemper, can be transmitted to such vulnerable puppies by anyone who has recently handled an infected or unprotected dog.

Those who work with orphaned puppies must wash their hands thoroughly before handling them. Any other dog in the home must never be allowed within the proximity of unprotected puppies under any circumstances whatsoever. If you handled any dog in the household, make certain you wash your hands again prior to going anywhere near the puppies, even if you just touch the knob on the door of the isolation room. Enough importance cannot be placed upon the value of the dam's colostrum, and as previously mentioned, puppies that have not received this form of protection are extremely vulnerable. Tape a KEEP OUT sign to the door of the puppy room as a constant reminder to everyone in your home. This can be the longest (and cleanest) six weeks you may ever experience.

Since chilling is the single greatest danger to the newborn puppies' survival, an incubator will have to be fashioned, as described earlier in this chapter. In this case, however, each puppy must be kept in its own separate compartment. This is particularly important with tube-fed puppies, because having no nipple on which to suck, they will suckle any part of a littermate's anatomy they can get into their mouths. If puppies are fed by nursing bottle, separating them becomes less critical, but it is still a good idea, as it is then possible to monitor with certainty the stools of each puppy—an extremely important indicator of how the puppies are faring. A thermometer should be placed in the incubator to monitor the surface temperature. Scrupulously change the soiled bedding constantly to avoid urine scalds. Maintain the temperature in the incubator at 85 to 90 degrees Fahrenheit for the first week. During the second week, reduce the temperature to 80 or 85 degrees and thereafter gradually decrease the temperature to 75 degrees by the end of the fourth week. Puppies are capable of regulating their own body heat by age three weeks. Maintain constant warmth and avoid chilling drafts at all times.

For those so inclined, there are excellent, commercially manufactured puppy incubators available. If you think you should own such a piece of equipment, consult your veterinarian on where to locate one.

HAND-FEEDING

If you are tube-feeding, the measurements you work with are likely to be metric (grams, ccs or mls). With bottle-feeding, the measurements are usually expressed in ounces. The following information may be useful in making up formulas and determining the amount to feed at each meal.

1 tablespoon = 17 mls
1 cup = 8 ounces/227 mls
1 ounce liquid = 28.3 mls
8 ounces liquid = 227 mls
1 ounce dry weight = 28.3 grams
1 pound dry weight = 453.5 grams

A newborn Bulldog puppy weighing eight ounces (227 grams) should be fed up to two and a half ounces (68 ml) of simulated bitch's milk per day, divided into six feedings of one-half ounce (14 ml) every four hours. If all proceeds well, the puppy can be expected to double its birth weight in the first ten days. Simple arithmetic tells you that the puppy that doubles its birth weight will need twice as much food, or one ounce (28 ml) of the milk at every feeding. Newborn Bulldog puppies may only be able to ingest a little over a quarter-ounce of milk at a time for the first two or three feedings. Also, as each puppy is an individual, some will take more than others and they will vary their individual intake with each feeding. Bear in mind that newborns normally tend to lose a small amount of weight in the first few hours following their birth, due to water depletion. After the third feeding, puppies will have recovered or exceeded their birth weight. Before and after feeding, all puppies must be made to eliminate, using cotton balls as described previously. While not being heavy-handed, it is not necessary to handle the puppies like champagne goblets. Their mother would be quite vigorous in this connection and some people marvel that a dam does not injure her puppies with their licking and roughhousing. After the puppies have been made to relieve themselves, they should be cleaned with a warm, damp cloth and returned to the incubator. This cleaning should include the anal area and the skin of the abdomen. A light application of baby oil should also be applied to these areas and to the coat to prevent the development of dry skin.

BOTTLE-FEEDING

Feeding Bulldog puppies with a baby bottle has a number of advantages over tube-feeding. First, the nipple satisfies the natural urge to suckle, while at the same time forces the puppy to perform his first regimen of exercise. Pulling at the nipple causes a puppy to use neck and shoulder muscles while kneading with the feet, thereby using the legs and indeed the entire body, stimulating increased appetite and enhanced growth. There is even an additional bonus to this as the puppy becomes familiar with the human hand, and so inadvertently begins the bonding process that will make him or her a wonderful companion for its entire life.

Any puppy weighing less than a pound quite obviously does not have the oral strength of a human baby. For this reason the opening in the soft nipple may not be large enough to allow an adequate flow of milk into the puppy's mouth. To remedy this, the hole in the nipple should be enlarged so that the milk will drip out *slowly* when the bottle is turned upside down. If a puppy has to struggle to feed, it will tire after just a few minutes of attempting to nurse and will not receive an adequate amount of food. Since puppies do not develop a gag reflex before they reach twenty-one days, care should be taken not to enlarge the opening in the nipple too much, as puppies may ingest too much food. Overeating is worse than getting too little. If a pup's belly gets too full, it will experience difficulty in breathing and may suffer a chill. Consequently, it is easy to understand why more puppies are lost to the effects of overfeeding than to underfeeding.

The best way to introduce a puppy to bottle-feeding is to place it on its stomach on a towel on your lap or over your crossed leg. The towel protects you in the event that the handling required stimulates the puppy to eliminate during the feeding session. Open the puppy's mouth with the tip of your finger, insert the nipple and hold the bottle up at about a 45-degree angle. The angle is to prevent any air from getting into the puppy's stomach. Periodically, pull the bottle gently away from the puppy as if to remove the nipple from its mouth, but without actually doing so. By doing this, you encourage vigorous sucking. In all cases, bottle-fed puppies must be burped after a feeding.

TUBE-FEEDING

This feeding method has a number of advantages over the others, but if not done correctly it can be disastrous. Feeding time per puppy is about two minutes. Air is not swallowed; consequently, burping is not required. The precise amount of formula required can easily be administered to each puppy. If puppies are sick, physiologically immature or too weak to nurse, tube-feeding is the only way they stand a chance of survival. With tube feeding also, all the guesswork goes out of administering liquid medications or supplements of any kind.

If too much formula is administered or if it is given too rapidly, the formula can flow back through the stomach into the mouth, causing the formula to be sucked into the lungs. The end result will be mechanical pneumonia. This dangerous complication can be avoided if care is taken to monitor the weight of the puppy so that the correct amount of formula is always provided as the puppy grows. Because tube-fed puppies do not get a chance to suckle at this early stage of their lives, they must be kept in separate compartments of the incubator.

To the uninitiated, the prospect of tube feeding can be understandably frightening, but it is not difficult to do and can be learned in a very few minutes. Ask your veterinarian or an experienced breeder friend to demonstrate the technique before you try it and have him or her with you at your first effort. The equipment required for tube feeding consists

Tube feeding: the inside story.—Rose Floyd
From *Dog Owner's Home Veterinary Handbook,* © 1992, 1980 by Howell Book House. Reproduced with permission.

of a No. 8 soft rubber catheter and a 20-cc syringe. As each puppy must have its own catheter, you will need a working supply as well as a good number of syringes. You can acquire these from a medical or kennel supply company. The catheters must be cleaned after each use and stored in plastic sandwich bags labeled with the identification of the puppy that uses it. If you have trouble finding this equipment, ask your veterinarian for help. The gram scale, mentioned earlier, is mandatory to monitor weight gains in any litter of puppies being tube-fed.

The Bulldog puppy's stomach is located at the level of the last rib. You must begin by measuring the tube from the mouth to the point of the last rib, following the contour of the head and body. You may have to be patient here as many puppies will squirm, so several attempts to get an accurate measurement may be necessary. Mark the tube with a tiny bit of tape near the mouth end which tells you when you have reached the stomach. Some of the newer tubes already have printed gradations on them, so if you can get these, you won't need to use tape. A small detail, of course, but in raising a litter, any little bit of help is good for the puppies and the care-giver.

If your catheters have belled ends, cut them off with sterile scissors so the tube will fit snugly over the syringe. Draw the exact amount of formula required for the puppy into the syringe, connect syringe and catheter and place the syringe in a small glass of warm water until the temperature reaches 100 degrees F. The tip of the catheter need not be immersed in the water. Holding up the tip of the catheter, depress the plunger on the syringe until the food material appears at the small openings at the other end of the catheter. This tells you that no air is present in the catheter. Moisten the tip of the tube with formula, gently open the puppy's mouth and pass the tube slowly over the tongue toward the ultimate objective. A puppy's tongue will always form an obliging "U"-shape when the formula is tasted, making the job of getting the tube on center much easier. The tube is too large to enter the smaller windpipe passage, so there is only a remote possibility of inserting the tube in the wrong spot. Use *slow, steady* pressure to insert the tube and the puppy will help you by swallowing it. Continue until the mark is at the puppy's mouth or until you meet resistance. If you do meet resistance, slowly withdraw the tube, give the puppy a moment to rest and try again. When the tube is safely in the puppy's stomach, *slowly* inject the formula. After a few days, your puppies should be strong enough to suckle from a bottle. If not, try a larger tube, as presumably the puppies have grown (or you would not still be feeding them) and you do not want to run the risk of inserting the tube into a puppy's lungs, which are a shorter distance from the mouth than the stomach.

COMMON FEEDING PROBLEMS

The most common problems are brought about from overfeeding and underfeeding and result in either diarrhea or a failure to gain weight. If puppies are gaining weight, passing normal, firm, yellowish stools and appear to be content, they are being fed the correct amount. Owners are much more likely to overfeed orphaned puppies as evidenced by the number of stools produced by each puppy. Six feedings a day should produce six or seven stools—about one per feeding. A loose, yellow stool generally indicates a mild degree of overfeeding and can be corrected by cutting back a little on the amount of formula.

135

With moderate overfeeding, there is a more rapid movement of food through the intestinal tract indicated by a greenish stool due to unabsorbed bile. Administering a couple of ccs of milk of magnesia every three hours and cutting back on the amount of formula usually corrects the problem.

Unchecked overfeeding leads to a depletion of digestive enzymes and causes a grayish, diarrheal stool. Eventually, when little or no digestion is taking place, the stool will resemble curdled milk. This is a serious matter, as the puppy is not getting any nutrition and is rapidly becoming dehydrated. This is a very serious condition and must be treated by diluting the formula by one-third, using previously boiled and cooled water combined with one to three ccs of milk of magnesia every three hours. The dehydration is corrected by administering via tube or nursing bottle about one cc of Pedialite per two ounces of body weight every hour. Ringers solution can also be administered by subcutaneous injection to treat dehydration. The proper amount is about two ccs spread over different parts of the body. All puppies passing gray or white stools should be taken to the veterinarian immediately to test for the presence of neonatal infection.

Puppies that do not get enough formula cry constantly. They appear listless and apathetic, gain little or no weight from one feeding to the next and eventually begin to get chilled. Under these circumstances the temperature should be checked and the heating pad should be looked at to make sure it is plugged in and working properly. If the bedding in the incubator is damp from not being changed often enough, it could chill the puppies with potentially lethal effects. Puppies dehydrate very quickly if they do not get enough formula. The necessary adjustments should be made to the diet and, hopefully, the puppies should fare much better.

Very young puppies that do not have normal bowel movements, or pass stool only occasionally compared to their siblings, will not fare well. If they do not eliminate body waste, they cannot accommodate normal food intake and their systems can become poisoned. A product that is useful for this problem, and readily available at pet stores, is Laxatone. This is actually a cat laxative and hairball remover that is very gentle and is safe for young puppies. Squeeze a little of this paste preparation on the tip of your small finger and allow the puppy to suck until it has all been ingested. This seems to work best when administered before feeding and a couple of doses usually gives the desired results.

An attractive pair of Bill and Kay Gray's Graybull puppies sired by Ch. Kerr's Winston Pride of Tugboat out of Ch. Li'l "OO" Trouble.

SWIMMERS

Swimmers are described as flat-bodied puppies that resemble turtles, with their legs sticking out to the sides rather than positioned normally underneath them. They are flat-chested while their littermates are up on all fours, albeit unsteadily. This condition is not uncommon in Bulldogs and is caused by a weakness of the muscles that pull the legs together. It can also lead to mild pneumonia, which can complicate the process of growing out of the defect.

Normal puppies begin to stand at about sixteen days old and exhibit a steady gait by the time they reach three weeks. If this is not happening with a given individual, that puppy may be a swimmer. Such a puppy will probably also be overweight compared to its siblings.

When puppies are first learning to walk, they must be provided with reliable traction. Understandably, smooth, slippery surfaces are bad for puppies and can lead to the development of swimmers, especially among overweight animals. Rubber-backed carpeting is a great deterrent to the development of the defect.

The usual remedy for correcting flat-chested swimmers is to hobble them with tape from elbow to elbow of the rear legs. Duct tape, torn into half-inch strips, tends to stay on the puppy longer. Before taping, gauze is wrapped around the area of the leg to be taped to avoid or minimize hair loss when the tape is removed. Several times a day, assist the swimmer to stand and walk. When the puppy stands, the hobble forces his rear legs to remain under him, and although he may appear temporarily ungainly when he walks, in most cases the puppy will be quite normal within a very few days. The hobble also makes it almost impossible for the puppy to sleep on his stomach, which will also help get him past this condition.

GRADING A LITTER

Some breeders can grade their litters immediately at birth, and can determine with almost absolute certainty the ultimate quality of each individual puppy at maturity. This is not unusual in closely linebred litters, where the breeder is very familiar with all the virtues and faults of the dogs and bitches named in the pedigree and even their forebears which no longer appear. Picking puppies *wet* is no different from choosing a puppy at eight weeks or eight months of age. One is in search of the best-balanced puppies in the litter, with the best heads, low ear sets, widest jaws, most bone, lowest tail sets, short backs and good ribbing. Generally speaking, the coat color of an individual will lighten a shade or two at about eight weeks. Markings often spread over a widened area from birth to eight weeks. For example, a small red dot against a white background on top of the head, between the ears, may proportionately cover three or four times the same area when the puppy reaches adult size.

BUYING A HEALTHY PUPPY

The usual age at which to buy a puppy is eight weeks. At this age it is possible for the astute breeder to determine whether or not a puppy is indeed a show prospect. However, even a breeder with considerable experience and a good track record in this regard can make a wrong

Jim Dutta's nine-week-old "Georgia" is the subject of this irresistible study in winsomeness.

prediction of an individual puppy's future worth as a winner. This is also a good age to ship a puppy to its new home. At this age puppies are formative and most new owners prefer to introduce their new pet into the normal routine of their family and commence training while the newcomer is still young and impressionable.

After having located several Bulldog breeders who have indicated that they have one or more puppies that could meet your requirements, you should let the breeder know that you are a good candidate to be a first-time Bulldog owner. The conscientious breeder will ask you about your home, family and living circumstances to satisfy him- or herself as to your suitability to acquire one of the puppies. However, you can also present yourself as the type of owner that would satisfy the most demanding Bulldog breeder. If you have a fenced yard with available shade, tell the breeder this. If your puppy would not have access to a yard, but would be exercised safely on a lead and get sufficient exercise in a nearby park, mention this, too. A Bulldog should not be made to spend all its time outdoors, so tell the breeder that you intend for yours to be a real member of the family, spending most of its time in the house. The presence of children in a family is an important factor to a breeder's decision to sell a puppy. If you have children, tell the breeder how many, their ages and

Yvonne and Mark Vogel's "Moose" at four months old, considering growing into his name. He was bred by John and Susan McGibbon.

sexes and whether they have been around animals. You will probably also be asked whether someone will be home during the day under normal circumstances during the puppy's period of development. If the breeder does not ask this, volunteer the information, because it really is important and in the best interests of the puppy.

If you want a dog you can show successfully, make this obvious. Don't try to economize on a show prospect by telling the breeder you only want a pet, hoping the breeder will make a mistake and sell you a future winner. She won't! If you buy a pet quality Bulldog and try showing it later, you will only succeed in looking ridiculous yourself and embarrassing the breeder in the process. Again, if the seller knows you want to show and perhaps breed, she can be enormously helpful and guide you in the best direction possible. If you have decided that you must have a dog of a certain color or are absolutely insistent on a dog or a bitch, mention any such requirements up front. In this way you will not waste the breeder's time or your own. If you decide to look at any breeder's puppies, make a firm appointment and be there on time. If your plans change and you can't make it, advise the breeder accordingly and reschedule. People can

This study of "Maybe Baby" after her bath earned her owner-photographer Dr. Sheila K. Neathery a second-place technical award of merit in a photo contest.

be amazingly inconsiderate of others when it comes to looking at puppies, and nothing grates on a breeder more than a "no-show."

Before you actually take delivery of a new puppy, locate a veterinarian who has worked with Bulldogs and is aware of their particular needs. Make the seller aware that you will be taking the puppy to this veterinarian within forty-eight hours for a thorough physical examination. The responsible breeder will be happy to hear this and may have already suggested you do so. In most cases, the breeder will give you two or three days to have your puppy examined by a veterinarian of your choice. If your vet finds some problem and suggests you return the puppy, this breeder will take the puppy back and give you a full refund of your purchase price. Once you have taken delivery, take the puppy directly to the vet, if at all possible, or at the first opportunity. Bulldog puppies are among the world's greatest heart stealers, so if a problem requiring the puppy's return is discovered, it can be emotionally wrenching to all concerned if you have held on to the puppy for any length of time. If you have the puppy checked within the time frame mentioned above, returning the puppy will be easier on all concerned.

Conscientious breeders are proud of their stock and will always be ready to stand behind their breeding. No one can guarantee that a young puppy, no matter how promising, will grow into a show dog. However, the care, training, feeding, health care and socialization of a puppy before and after it goes to a new home are every bit as important as the genetic makeup of all its ancestors.

If you visit a breeder to make your selection, don't panic when you find yourself standing ankle deep in the middle of a litter of bouncing Bulldog puppies as they pull on your shoelaces and anything else they can reach. They will all appear equally lovable and healthy at first glance. However, don't be rushed—a closer examination may reveal some factor that may render a given puppy less desirable than it seemed at first glance. If the breeder shows you several puppies to pick from, take your time and be sure that the puppy you take is the one you really want.

PHYSICAL EXAMINATION

Every owner of a Bulldog should know how to conduct a physical examination to check a dog's overall health, to look for any injury or external problem and, in so doing, be better able to communicate with the veterinarian in any eventuality. Conducting a proper physical is even more important for the owner of a puppy, as the health status of a young animal can change in an instant and it helps to know what you are dealing with.

To examine a Bulldog puppy, start with the animal facing you. The nose should be cool and moist, although a dry nose by itself is not a sign of illness. Gently squeeze the nostrils together to see if any mucous is present. A nasal discharge or frequent sneezing suggests a possible infection of the respiratory tract. The nostrils should be open when the dog inhales. Remember that a Bulldog's nostrils are an extremely important feature. They should be large, wide and black with a well-defined median line between them. It is not unusual for Bulldogs to be born with flesh-colored nostril pigment. However, any puppy with such pigment at age eight weeks may never fully blacken and may be a candidate for a pet home.

The gums should be pink and healthy-looking. If the tip of a finger is pressed against a gum, the spot will turn white, but returns to its normal color almost immediately following the finger being withdrawn. This response is called *capillary refill* and is a helpful health check. If gums do remain white when they should "pink up," the attention of a veterinarian may be required.

A Bulldog's eyes should look straight ahead and not deviate to the side. If discolored areas due to tear stains are present on the dog's muzzle, look for eyelids that turn in (entropion) or out (ectropion), extra eyelashes or conjunctivitis. White spots on the surface of the eye could be scars from previous injuries or infections. The pupils should be dark and show no visible lines or white spots. Juvenile cataracts or retained fetal membranes may interfere with vision. In Bulldogs the haw and the third eyelid may be visible where they would not be in other breeds of dogs. These are not necessarily signs of illness unless accompanied by swelling or inflammation.

The ear canals should be clean, dry and completely free of any unpleasant odor. An accumulation of wax accompanied by a rancid smell may signal the presence of ear mites. Repeated head shaking and tenderness about the ears are your clue to suspect an infection is present in one or both ear canals.

Feel the puppy's chest with the palm of your hand to determine whether or not the chest feels especially vibrant compared to those of other puppies. Young Bulldog puppies tend to have a more rapid heart rate at eight weeks than puppies of other breeds. Breathing should be effortless. A flat chest, especially when accompanied by labored inhalation, may indicate an airway obstruction. As a test, gently pinch the windpipe. This action should not trigger a coughing spasm. If it does, the puppy may be suffering from bronchitis.

The skin of the abdomen should be clean and exhibit a healthy appearance. A bulge at the navel is probably the result of an umbilical hernia. This condition is not uncommon in Bulldogs and is easily repaired. A bulge in the groin indicates an inguinal hernia, the repair of which is more involved than that of an umbilical hernia.

In examining a male puppy, push the foreskin back to confirm that it slides back and forth easily. Adhesions between the prepuce and the head of the penis, as well as strictures of the foreskin, require veterinary attention. Both testicles should be about the same size and normally descended in the scrotum. A dog with only one testicle is called

The author with his eight-week-old JB Rare Moses at the Pacific Coast Bulldog Club match. This promising puppy was photographed on this occasion by his proud breeder, Libby Moses.

a *monorchid* and is ineligible to compete in the showring and should not be used for breeding. A dog with neither testicle descended is called a *cryptorchid*, and it, too, is ineligible for competition. A puppy

JB Rare Maribeth with her four-hour-old litter.

showing either condition should be altered to avoid any possibility of development of testicular malignancy later in life. However, before the inguinal ring closes, young puppies can sometimes pull up their testicles when they are cold or frightened. Therefore it is important to be sure that a puppy is just pulling up his testes at times rather than exhibiting the nature of a true monorchid. For a show or breeding prospect, it can be disastrous to give up too soon and castrate an otherwise potential winner.

Female puppies should be examined for any pasted-looking hair or unusual discharge at the vulva. This generally indicates juvenile vaginitis, a common problem requiring appropriate treatment, as prescribed by your veterinarian.

The skin and hair around the anus should also be clean and healthy looking. Any signs of irritation, such as redness and hair loss, indicate the possibility of worms, chronic diarrhea or a digestive disorder. The coat should be bright, shiny and clean. Any obvious scale, itching or deposits of dirt in the coat suggests fleas, mites or other parasites—external or internal. The appearance of a moth-eaten coat or areas of hair loss are typical symptoms of mange or ringworm. Any dog so affected should be seen by a veterinarian at the earliest possible time. Obviously, a puppy buyer who is offered an individual showing these symptoms should look elsewhere.

Now is the time for the prospective buyer to examine the puppy for soundness and correct structure. The inner sides of the front legs should be straight and well-formed. The puppy should be examined for legs that bow in or out, weak pasterns, flat feet with spread toes or front or hind feet that toe in. The puppy's gait should be free, smooth and elastic and the whole animal should be alert, active, playful and teeming with vitality. A Bulldog puppy typically has a sweet disposition. By contrast, an aggressive puppy is very undesirable. If offered such a puppy, never consider it, especially in a home that includes children or senior citizens. Shy puppies may be a headache to train and may be difficult or even impossible to socialize.

Ideally, a well-adjusted puppy will follow people around enthusiastically and accept attention readily. The puppy may struggle when first picked up, but soon relaxes and seeks to lick the hand of the person holding him. Good health and correct temperament usually go hand-in-hand, so the wisest course may be to choose the best conformed puppy that is also bursting with vitality, enthusiasm and confidence in its world.

Once you have settled on your own puppy, you should always be able to depend on the wise counsel of the breeder. This support will be particularly critical in the first few weeks with the puppy in your home. Any guarantees concerning the puppy you have decided to buy should be discussed in detail and committed to in writing before the sale is finalized. At the time of sale you should also receive either the puppy's registration certificate properly signed over to you or registration application, also properly signed over. You will also be given a pedigree, health certificate and a record of all inoculations, wormings and other veterinary care the puppy has received up to the time you acquired it. Finally, the

Bulldog puppies love everyone. —Photo courtesy of Dr. Sheila K. Neathery.

conscientious breeder will include a diet sheet and a small supply of the food to which the puppy is accustomed. This will tide the puppy over until you can purchase your own supply of the same food or gradually switch it to a diet you prefer.

Breeding fine dogs involves pride and the sincere Bulldog breeder wants you to be happy with your puppy. He or she is always ready to help and advise. The bond doesn't break when the puppy goes home with you, and that is the beauty and comfort of acquiring a well-bred, well-reared Bulldog puppy from a true friend of the breed.

JB Rare Max Factor, bred and owned by John and Susan McGibbon.

CHAPTER 9

Living with Bulldogs: Some Helpful Hints

THIS CHAPTER WAS WRITTEN PRIMARILY WITH BULLDOGS IN MIND, BUT THE suggestions that follow actually apply to all dogs. Dog fanciers seem to have a facility for applying anything that they read or hear toward bettering the lives of dogs and their owners. Most of the suggestions contained in this chapter have been used successfully at one time or another by the author. However, if you use the advice that follows, do so with discretion; no guarantees are expressed or implied with any of this.

FLEAS

The old song, *"My Dog Has Fleas,"* is funny, but flea infestation is not. Any dog can have fleas at one time or another; however, by using the following techniques, we have found that on the rare occasion that we must deal with these insidious parasites, simple table salt can stop fleas before they can wreak total havoc. On those occasions when an infested

Ch. Chile Patch Eloise, owned by Brett Duncan.

canine visitor to our home left behind enough fleas to found an entire new colony, we would simply sprinkle the table salt liberally in the areas the visitor occupied, particularly carpet and furnishings. The salt does not damage the carpet or furniture fabric, in our experience. Leave the salt on for at least twenty-four hours, then vacuum. The fleas will be gone. In the case of a major infestation, such as following an outing to a dog show, or the visit of an infested dog whose condition is not realized until several days after its departure, the same ritual is performed again after ten days in order to kill any fleas from newly hatched eggs. Now the fleas are really eliminated. So, you ask, how do we keep fleas out of the house or kennel, off of our dogs, away from the garage, the yard and any other area we really want to keep clean? The entire war on fleas—if you are to become victorious—depends on your being consistent. If fleas are on the dog and not on the carpet, be assured that this condition is very temporary. The same applies to the yard and garage or kennel. *All must be treated at the same time, as follows:*

1. Bathe your dog(s), then flea dip.

2. Salt the entire area. A couple of pounds should cover an average house. Same applies to the yard and garage or kennel.

3. Using a lawn and garden hose with a standard, eight-ounce sprayer attachment, add two ounces of household bleach to the bottle, then add an equal amount of water and set the concentration to about one-and-a-half ounces per gallon. Turn on the water hose with the sprayer attached and go to it. The amount recommended will cover about one thousand square feet and doesn't seem to damage grass or plants. Our dog run is treated this way every eight to ten days year-round, and it is still green, requiring mowing on a regular basis.

   An additional benefit to this bleach spray is that ants, spiders and other unwanted pests also temporarily disappear. The bleach also tends to discourage Parvovirus. Bulldog bitches in season seem to be more prone to bladder infections than other breeds, probably due to their low-slung anatomy and swollen tissues touching the ground. Using the bleach spray may well be beneficial in reducing infections by reducing the presence of potentially harmful organisms.

4. Wherever we transport our dogs, we only use our van for the purpose, and there is always a layer of salt on the carpet. This is optional, of course.

5. Prevention is better than cure. The addition of garlic to the dogs' daily food dish also seems to be beneficial. In Southern California we have warm, dry weather about ten months a year. Thus, it can be a never-ending battle with fleas, but not to those of us who feed a little garlic to our dogs each and every day. Some owners just add a little chopped garlic sprinkled on the kibble, others prefer more of a gourmet approach. I simmer about one-half inch of water in a two-quart pan, then add a teaspoon of garlic powder—*not garlic salt*—and a few sprinkles of dried parsley. I allow the concoction to brew for two or three minutes, then add cold water, allow to cool and divide it among the dogs by pouring it over their dry food. I know that they enjoy garlic because on those occasions that I neglect to follow the foregoing procedure, I get baleful glances and am punished by half-eaten meals. Apparently fleas do not like dogs with garlic in their blood. The quantities given are sufficient for four dogs. The purpose of the parsley? It greatly reduces the volatile effects of the garlic on the dogs' breath.

Ch. Breckley's Little Candy Gram, owned by Kenneth Haeflinger and bred by Al and Peggy Breckley.

Ch. Benjamin's Big Max of Pedley, bred and owned by Ben and Barbara Hill.

BITCHES IN SEASON

Not too long ago, we had a phone call from a lady who had bought a bitch from us three years previously. This lady has an immaculate home, beautiful antique furniture, not a speck of dust and everything in its place. In previous seasons her "baby" wore *bitches' britches*. However, this time we had bred her and she had a litter of five puppies. We accompanied them to the vet and to her home as this was the first litter for both of them. We stayed for a few hours to be sure that all was well, then left for home. Later that evening came the call—*your bitch* has bled all over my spotless white-nap carpet. What to do? "Very simple resolution to the problem," I said. "Do you have 10 percent hydrogen peroxide? Fine, then pour it on the bloody area and forget about it." She did, and it was gone in the morning without a trace of stain. This always works.

Dorothy Rumbo of La-Nan-Dor's Bulldogs with three-month-old Ms. Rumbo, who represents four decades of breeding.—Olan Mills

OTHER CARPET STAINS

In any household where dogs and people live together, the most common type of carpet stain is caused by urine. Happily, there is also an easy remedy for these stains.

The normal reaction after witnessing the family dog urinating on the carpet is to use paper towels, which are placed over the affected area. At this point the usual procedure is to stomp on the towels as if one were making wine. *Wrong*. All this does is to remove a small volume of fluid from the surface, while effectively forcing the noxious liquid into the underpad where it will remain forever, all the while reminding everyone in "sniffing distance" of its presence even after drying. Always—always—especially when puppies are around, have on hand a good supply of cornstarch. Do not use paper towels; just sprinkle the cornstarch on top of and around the wet area. Be sure to use enough, at least a quarter of an inch thick and about half an inch wider in diameter than the stain itself. Leave it in place for at least twenty-four hours, and if an adult dog was the perpetrator, then wait twice as long. The cornstarch will turn yellow and will appear to be caked. Vacuum it up. There will be no stain and no odor, and the dogs will not return to this spot.

The cornstarch treatment works on any color and any type of carpet fabric. I have been told by former dog owners that had they been aware of this simple solution, they would still own their dog. Well, maybe.

DIARRHEA

What an offensive word this is, and how well it matches the offensive effluent it designates. The stains from diarrhea are not nearly as easy to clean up as the urine spots. The problem is of course caused by visitors' dogs, never your own. They are, therefore, more distasteful and more difficult to eradicate. First, if you find one occurrence, look for another—they tend to materialize in twos and threes. Again, smother the stool in cornstarch, and this time cover with a paper towel that has been soaked in Pine Sol. Both the cornstarch and the disinfectant/deodorizer are beneficial, one to dry it up as quickly as possible, and the other to allow you to remain in the house. Change the paper towel as frequently as needed, but patience is required; the siege may last a week. Ultimately the *pancake* you have fashioned will become flat and very dry. I leave it to your

Am., Can. Ch. T-Town Jazz Man, No. 2 Bulldog in the United States for 1994, is owned by B. and S. Walter.—J. Cirincione

own devices as to how to remove the larger portion, but for the remainder use a wire slicker brush, available wherever pet supplies are sold.

Briskly pull the brush through the pile of the carpet in every direction, and wear a handkerchief over your nose and mouth as you will be creating fecal dust. Have your vacuum close by, and if you have the canister type, keep it running adjacent to the work area to eliminate as much dust as possible. When you are satisfied that you have it all, spray with Pine Sol as necessary.

SHAMPOOS

There are many excellent, expensive dog shampoos on the market, most of which also claim to rid your dog of fleas, lice and other external parasites. The process has to be repeated in about ten days in order to kill any eggs that hatched since the first bathing to totally disrupt the life cycle and be rid of the pests. But because you are now using the regimen described earlier, it makes no sense to spend money unnecessarily, when

Shi Mar, a Best of Breed winner at thirteen months, owned by Donna Dillard.

a perfectly pH balanced substitute is available for roughly 10 percent of the cost of commercial shampoos, in the same way that the cost of household bleach compares to malathion.

About ten years ago a professor of canine dermatology at Davis School of Veterinary Medicine pointed out that if the shampoo can kill fleas (which are about the longest surviving creatures on this planet), then what can it do to a dog? Careful dog keepers know enough not to flea dip a bitch in whelp—food for thought? My preferred substitute is Palmolive dishwashing liquid, as recommended by the good professor.

CHEWING, AND OTHER NO-NO'S

There is a commercial dog product on the market that is recommended, but not for its stated purpose. Grannick's Bitter Apple is sold as a coat spray that stops dogs from chewing their hair. Puppies, on the other hand, will chew almost anything that you treasure. Remember the antique chair that you used to be so proud of? When puppies are outside with all of their approved toys, they still gnaw on the door frames and anything else they can get their jaws on. Use "Bitter Apple" spray on any vulnerable areas in the morning, and the puppies will leave them alone. After a few days of this practice, they decide that they really don't like to chew, or at least they don't like to chew on the surfaces you have treated. This is a lesson that stays with the puppies for life. In the case of furniture, do not spray directly onto the wood or fabric; instead spray the product on rags or paper towels, and when dry, wrap around the area to be protected. The dog will not go near your treasure. As of this writing, we have been looking after a five-year-old bitch in our home for a friend, for about three weeks. "Delilah" prefers the lap of luxury and is normally accustomed to sleeping in her owner's bed and reclining on any furniture she selects. Not in our house, Delilah! I sprayed four strips of paper towel with Bitter Apple, and when they were dry, I laid them on the sofa. I am happy to report that "Delilah" now sleeps on the floor alongside the sofa and the strips were used for only two days.

INTERDIGITAL CYSTS

Regarding this subject, I asked my colleague, Jack Brown of Jack-Pott Bulldogs to share his experiences in this matter. His remarks follow later in this section.

For many years I had been led to believe that these cysts were caused by an organism similar to the demodectic mange mite. Over the years the treatments espoused have included soaking the feet in Clorox bleach or feminine douches, oral medication, laser surgery, cryogenic surgery, and making a serum from blood drawn from the cyst.

At a Bulldog Club of America national Specialty show a few years ago, a dog I had with me had an interdigital cyst, and Jack was kind enough to treat it. The next morning, the first thing I noticed was that the area between the toes was no longer red and swollen. When the dog stood up in his crate, the cyst burst and blood flowed profusely. The following day the dog walked normally, and the problem did not recur.

Ch. Kaysinger's Shameless Betty, owned by Oman and Genevieve Kaysinger.

INTERDIGITAL CYSTS

H. Jack Brown, M.D., F.A.C.S.

Interdigital cysts are not true cysts but an abscess (collected pus) around a foreign body. The foreign body is usually a loose hair that has broken off and worked itself into the skin between the toes, but may be a grass spike or burr. A similar condition commonly occurs as an occupational hazard among barbers and hairdressers. The only cure is complete surgical excision of all inflamed tissue and meticulous suturing to close the dead space (wound cavity). A useful remedy is a half-and-half mixture of DMSO gel and Panolog prescription. DMSO is an anti-inflammatory agent, but more importantly, is a carrying agent that will be absorbed through the skin into the infected wound cavity,

Ch. Burly Hollows Dudley Tat, owned and bred by Jerry and Susie Bennett.

taking the Panolog prescription with it. Apply twice a day until all inflammation has subsided. Oral antibiotics will go only so far as the blood stream carries them, and do not, therefore, get to the center of infection that has become a cavity. The earlier this treatment is begun the more successful it is. Large neglected lesions must first be incised and drained. Puncturing the cyst with a needle is inadequate. Remember, the DMSO-Panalog combination is not a cure, but treats the acute infection. The underlying cause (the foreign body) is still present and will cause the problem to recur.

GROOMING

The customary grooming admonishments are to bathe, brush and clean your dogs' face and wrinkles on a regular basis. However, the tear stains on a Bulldog's face are particularly difficult to eradicate. The stains are not only unsightly, but in extreme cases can become infected. "Desitin," an ointment commonly used to treat diaper rash and other skin conditions, readily available in pharmacies and supermarkets, is the best treatment available for tear stains. Start at the corner of the eye, and smear a heavy layer of the ointment along the length of the stain. The dog will make every attempt to wipe the ointment off by rubbing his face on the carpet. Be consistent, and in two or three weeks the stain will be gone and hair will begin to regrow. Once you have the problem eradicated, a light application, as needed, will keep the stains at bay. If you are an exhibitor, do not apply the ointment close to a dog show date, as Desitin is very difficult to remove. That's one of the reasons it works so well.

It is not unusual to see Bulldogs with crusty, even wartlike noses. Petroleum jelly is commonly used for show dogs' noses as a minor cosmetic. However, extreme cases are candidates for "Panolog." Squirt a quarter-inch of the ointment on the nose, gently rub it in, repeat two or three times a day, and within a week or less the nose will be normally smooth and black.

To remove dead hair that routine brushing just doesn't seem to get, use a lava brick. This item that has a characteristically strong odor of sulfur and is readily available from barbecue supply stores really does the job. The brick is very light in weight, porous, and can be cut with a breadknife

"Somehow these guys always make me feel stuffed." Life is good for the resident Bulldog at the home of Arlene and Larry Siegal.

or old hacksaw blade. A convenient size would be about that of a bar of bath soap. Brush the coat as usual, then, with short quick strokes, starting at the neck, go over the entire coat. If you have a dog with a white collar that has a few stray hairs that impinge upon the adjacent colored sections of the coat, use the corner of the brick to scoop the white hairs away. No scissors marks will show—and a perfect blend will be the final, pleasing result. Due to the air that is now available to the skin as a result of your grooming, the formerly beautiful coat will soon be spectacular.

ARTHRITIS

Arthritis is as common in dogs as it is in people. Although aspirin is a useful remedy for people, this is not the case when administered to dogs. Aspirin can, and often does eat away at the canine stomach lining with sometimes disastrous results—therefore, do not give your dog even baby aspirin. A decidedly off-beat remedy that is usually very effective both in humans and in dogs, and there is no explanation why, is made by

162

soaking "golden raisins" in gin. Yes, gin! Cover the raisins (and they can *only* be golden raisins) in gin in a tumbler and allow to marinate overnight. The raisins soak up the liquor and can be added to the dogs' food the next day. The addition of two or three of these "drunken raisins" in a dog's food each day will begin to show results in a week or ten days. This is also good for the young show dog that is going through growing pains and only limps in the showring, but stops limping forever after successfully completing its championship.

ANASARCA (WATER) PUPPIES

Many human medications can safely be given to dogs in much larger doses than would seem appropriate when considering the difference in weight between a person and a Bulldog. A good example is the use of human diuretics in pregnant Bulldog bitches that are carrying excess water in their bodies. The expectation is that all or part of the litter will be born as Anasarca (water) puppies. The use of diuretics on pregnant Bulldog bitches has been successfully employed, using the same dosage as one would on a two-hundred-pound person. One must, however, be certain to replace the potassium and other important minerals the bitch is eliminating from her system. At about four weeks into the pregnancy turn the bitch over and examine the areolas (the flat portion of skin that forms the base of each nipple). If the color appears to be an opalescent light blue, then in all probability the bitch is carrying water puppies, especially if her belly is unusually tight for this stage of her pregnancy. If the diuretic is administered as described, accompanied by the appropriate metal salts, then a normal pregnancy and delivery can be anticipated.

PUTTING WEIGHT ON DOGS

Most of us have had dogs that look wonderful around the house and backyard. They are living a normal, reasonably stress-free life. The first dog show of the season is a few weeks away and preparation and conditioning time is at hand. Whisker trimming, nail grinding, additional exercise sessions, more brushing than normal, and more private time with the family become part of the daily routine. The dog loses weight as its normal regimen is sharply altered.

"Bogie," owned by Nancy Elliott, turns on the charm as only a well-loved Bulldog can.

The following mixture of ingredients seems to work in almost all cases with Bulldogs who go off their food, losing weight and vitally important condition when you would least want them to do.

Troybev's Bohemian Rhapsody, owned by Beverly and Troy Smith, Sr.

"FAT BALLS" CONDITIONING SUPPLEMENT

10 pounds cheap, fat ground beef

12 packets Knox unflavored gelatin

1 dozen eggs

1 large box Total breakfast cereal, crushed in the box

1 quart molasses

1 quart wheat germ

Knead the mixture thoroughly by hand until you have created a sticky blend.

All Bulldoggers have scales with which to weigh their puppies, so weigh out the "fat ball" mixture into one-pound fractions, thereby producing about fourteen segments. Roll the meat mixture into "meat balls" of approximately one and a quarter inches in diameter, place them in plastic bags and store them in the freezer. Defrost in the morning as much as you plan to use each day by switching the required supply from the freezer to the refrigerator, and feed the "Fat Balls" immediately before the regular meal. It normally takes a dog about four days before the results become noticeable—a Bulldog that normally will weigh fifty-five pounds will gain four pounds in about nine days. This excessively high-fat, high-protein, potentially unhealthy formulation is not recommended as a daily diet, but it is useful for assisting the weight retention of dogs that have a tendency to dislike the showring but that are worthy of attaining their championship titles. It is fairly common that dogs and bitches who have been weight losers prior to becoming champions never have the problem again after the fact. This, I assume, is entirely due to the anxiety of the owners, which is transferred to the dogs, hence causing the loss of weight and condition.

CHAPTER
10

Training, Showing and Judging Bulldogs

TRAINING A BULLDOG STARTS AS SOON AS YOU BRING YOUR NEW PUPPY HOME. First, he has to learn as fast as possible that he must be clean around the house, and to understand that the place to answer the call of nature is outdoors. At the final stage of raising puppies, most breeders provide an area of the whelping box that is covered in paper. They also have a rug or blanket area that is heated by a lamp or heating pad. It follows that the pups will not mess up the heated area where they sleep, but will instead avail themselves of the newspaper. If the breeder, by some chance, has not instructed the new owner in house-training the puppy, then the following should be useful advice.

Decide in advance which door you want the dog to use to get to the backyard, and place the newspaper in front of, and almost touching the door. Immediately upon entering the room, place the puppy on the newspaper and stay with him until he appears to be ready to eliminate. When the obvious signs are unmistakable, open the door and gently push the puppy over the threshold; do not pick the puppy up and place him

167

Ch. Hug-O-Bull's Ridgefield Calypso, owned and bred by Frank, Norma and Elizabeth Hugo, had an Award of Merit at the Bulldog Club of America's National Specialty in 1987 and was Best of Opposite Sex at the same event in 1988.

Ch. Tsar's Fat Man's Finale, owned and bred by Jim and Zoya Cardello, was Best of Breed at the BCA National Specialty in 1991.

outside. He has to learn that he must make the transition from inside to outside by himself. It normally takes about two days for the puppy to get the idea, so be patient. If you catch the puppy attempting to use a part of the room, don't become upset and scream at him. Firmly say, "No," then place the puppy on the newspaper and repeat the procedure described above. If necessary, get out the cornstarch and use the remedy given for accidents in the previous chapter.

SELECTING THE PERFECT NAME

You are naturally anxious to have your dog answer to whichever name that you have chosen for him or her. Puppies normally have about a ten- to fifteen-second attention span, so never use the chosen name when issuing a correction. "No" is all that you should say, because if you use the dog's name, as in "Max—No," the dog will become confused, not understanding what you mean. The dog's name is normally used affectionately, and the "No" is used sternly with a different tone of voice. The dog should not have his name used in the same breath as a command. So when a correction is called for—just say "No."

One of the most popular names for a dog is "Max." Other names in this category are Duke, Shadow, Brandy, Sam, Lady, Molly, and so on. It would seem to be a good idea to choose a name that fits the dog's individual personality or "ethnic" background. An excellent sourcebook for suitable names is *When Rover Just Won't Do* (1993, Howell Book House) written by Danny Scalisi and Bulldog breeder Libby Moses. In this highly recommended book, you will find a choice of over two thousand names, many wonderfully unique, together with their derivations.

Ch. Kerr's Winston Pride of Tugboat, owned by Robert and Lenora Kerr, was Best of Breed at the 1987 BCA National Specialty and returned in 1993 to be named Best Veteran.—Missy Yuhl

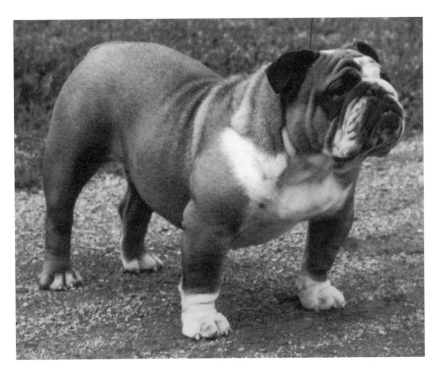

Ch. Bowag's Rosebud Day, owned and bred by Beverly and O'Neill Wagner.

COLLAR AND LEAD

Before you bring the puppy home, or certainly within a few days of its arrival, obtain a suitably sized collar. Be sure that it is not too big for the puppy's neck, to avoid the possibility that it will get caught on an impediment and choke the wearer. At this age it is also wisest to select an inexpensive collar. The explosive growth of a young Bulldog puppy makes the purchase of a fine collar ill-advised until your dog is just about finished growing.

The puppy will soon become accustomed to wearing the collar, and will become totally oblivious to its presence. Take the puppy to the backyard and run around with it, encouraging it to run toward you. Once the pup gets the idea, and begins to enjoy these play sessions, attach a light lead to the collar, and allow the dog to walk, run and play with the lead on, without you personally holding the other end. The next step, in a day or two, is to encourage the pup to walk in the yard with you holding the lead very loosely, but you go where the dog goes, praising him all the while. Do not attempt to pull the pup in any direction other than where he wants to go. Little by little, day by day, make him aware that you are exercising more and more control. Within a week, you will have a puppy that is happy to be with you, on a lead, because the training was a pleasurable, positive experience for you both. All aspects of dog training should be approached with the same attitude, whether your Bulldog buddy is getting your newspaper or your slippers, extending his paw for a handshake, rolling over or learning to stay on command.

TRAINING THE FUTURE SHOW DOG

Training a dog for the showring should start at the same time as lead training, but remember that an eight-week-old puppy tires very readily, so limit your joint training sessions to about five minutes. There is no harm done by conducting several short sessions a day and this approach is better than trying a single extended one. The Bulldog's outward appearance belies his considerable intelligence. Actually a Bulldog can be taught to do anything any other dog of any other breed can do; the difference is that a Bulldog is better at training its owners than are other dogs. However, the Bulldog also has a very well-developed stubborn streak.

The first objective in show training is to teach the puppy to stand. The same patience must be exercised as with lead training. A gentle but firm voice and equally gentle hands will also make this part of the dog's education more pleasurable for those at either end of the lead. We must always bear in mind that the only reason Bulldogs exist at all is to provide pleasure to people. A proportionately small number of the Bulldogs in our midst will go on to compete in the showring, and they will do so at the behest of the owners, not the dogs. The Bulldog you are trying to prepare for the showring is doing you the favor, and trying its best to please. Accordingly, it would be a mistake to become distressed if all does not go well during those first few training sessions. The dog will sense that you have become exasperated, and will not regard training and showing as an enjoyable experience. The dog's performance in the ring will ultimately reflect this.

For the actual instruction, place the show prospect on a low table with a rough towel or nonskid mat for him to stand on. At this age he only weighs ten or twelve pounds, and is easily manageable. As he is off

Ch. Smasher's Al Capp, owned by Karl Foerster (handling), Ray Knudson and Caroline Whiteside, was a well-known winner on the breed and Group level.—Phoebe

the floor and in your hands, this ensures his undivided attention. He should be wearing his collar, but not the lead. Simply hold him in place, without concern for foot positioning, provided that he is standing comfortably and well balanced, with one hand on his chest, the other cupping his rear. While holding this position for ten or fifteen seconds, continuously repeat *stand* or *hold*, or any word with which you feel comfortable. Speak softly and clearly, and before he has time to get fidgety, praise him joyfully. Show your pleasure for a brief interval—fifteen seconds or so—then repeat the process several times before ending the session on a high note. After a few sessions, your Bulldog puppy will be accustomed to standing still, so now you can take hold of the collar, and, while still controlling his rear, continue to tell him to stand with a pleased inflection in your voice. Again, when he has passed this part of the *stacking* training, you can now progress to placing his feet, sometimes holding his collar, and sometimes with your finger under his chin. By this time you should be placing yourself only on the dog's right side. This is the position you will take in the ring when you present your dog to the judge. As in all training, continue praising your puppy for his good performance all the while.

In the showring, dogs are evaluated in motion as well as standing still. There are several standard gaiting patterns judges use to measure soundness as well as correct movement for the particular breed. The Bulldog's distinctive gait is very important to the whole picture, and it is essential to have your puppy trained to move so that his normal gait can be compared to the dictates of the Standard. The usual gaiting patterns are the circle, the down and back, the triangle and the "L." The names describe the way the dogs are to move and the judge will instruct you as to his or her preference. For more complete information, you are advised to acquire and study *Dog Showing: An Owner's Guide* and *The Winning Edge: Show Ring Secrets*, both published by Howell Book House.

PUTTING IT ALL TOGETHER

It's time now to combine all of the show training, walking on the lead with your dog on your left only, stopping and stacking—setting him up, commanding him gently to stand, gaiting up and back in a straight line,

Ch. Harjo's Miracle Babe, owned and handled by Dave Williams.

a circle making triangles and "L"-shapes, all on a loose lead. While your star pupil is set up, have a friend run hands over the puppy and open his mouth, look in his ears, check his eyes, and in the case of a male, gently touch the testicles.

The best experience that you and your puppy can get, inexpensively, is at puppy matches. If you cannot find matches advertised in your local

Ch. Big Ben Stoutheart, owned and bred by Clyde and Betty Anderson, was returned to his breeders at age six. His show career was begun soon afterward and he attained his championship when he was almost seven years old.—Cott/Francis

newspapers, ask your puppy's breeder for guidance. Matches are for fun, and training for both dog and owner. Your dog gets to meet others under controlled circumstances; he walks around the ring in the circle with the other puppies, and is judged individually by a total stranger. Often the person that is judging has little or no experience with Bulldogs, so don't worry if your pup doesn't come out the winner. You are at the match to practice, have fun and meet others with Bulldogs. Always remember that the most successful exhibitors think as much of their dogs after judging is over as they did before it started, regardless of the results.

SOCIALIZING THE FUTURE SHOW DOG

As your puppy reaches the age of four or five months, he can now be taken for short walks in the neighborhood, always on a lead and under your control. Perhaps you may enjoy visiting public parks that cater to dogs or malls and shops that welcome them. The more people that your puppy meets under a variety of different circumstances, who pet and make a fuss of him (normal for Bulldogs), the better a companion and show dog he will become. Bulldogs do not fare well in hot weather, so do your walking when the temperature is suitable or in climate-controlled surroundings. Dog show venues present a challenging variety of different surfaces, so walk your hopeful on grass, concrete, blacktop, linoleum, rubber or plastic runners, or any other skid-proof surfaces you can find. When you get to the "big time," the more prepared you and your dog are, the better you will be able to concentrate on showing your dog to its best advantage.

THE BIG STEP TO POINT SHOWS

Point shows are so designated for the championship points that can be won at them. Before entering your first point show, a visit without your dog to a couple of similar events in the local area would be very beneficial. These shows, sponsored by area kennel clubs, are usually mounted by a professional dog show superintendent who handles all the physical details of the event. Many are major productions, sometimes with as many as three thousand dogs entered. While visiting a show, you will be able to pick up premium lists and entry blanks for future shows at the superintendent's office. This would also be a good time to fill out a card that will get you on the superintendent's mailing list. Once on the mailing list, you will receive premium lists for future shows on a regular basis. The premium lists are mailed to all prospective exhibitors about two

Ch. Kozabull Glynbourne Zeke, bred by P. DiBello and Claire Tomlinson and owned by Ms. Tomlinson with Ed and Jean Kozatek. A member of the BCA Hall of Fame, "Zeke" is a celebrated producer as well as a multiple Specialty and Group winner.—Chuck Tatham

months prior to the actual show date. The premium list indicates all the information needed to enter and get to the show, including the show date and exact location, the entry fee and the closing date, after which date no entry can be accepted, and includes several entry blanks. There will also be listings of the names, addresses and assignments of all judges, listings of any special prizes, show rules and other items of particular importance to exhibitors.

Ch. Millcoat's Maximum Yardley, a Best in Show and multiple Specialty winner, owned by Nancy Rose, DVM, and Bob and Brenda Newcomb.—Petrulis

Gone is the relaxed, leisurely atmosphere of those puppy matches you have now become familiar with. At some shows you may have to park a considerable distance from the actual showing area. You may have to wend your way between crates and other exhibitors in the grooming area, push your way between handlers hurrying with their dogs to their rings, trip over tent lines and negotiate past concession booths. It can be total bedlam, so leave for these shows much earlier than you would normally depart for a match. At most outdoor shows, Bulldogs will be scheduled first thing in the morning when it is usually still cool and damp. It took many years to convince the show-giving clubs that the cooler hours are the safer hours for Bulldogs to be shown. The courtesy is greatly appreciated by all Bulldog enthusiasts.

HOW A DOG BECOMES A CHAMPION

For a dog or bitch to attain championship status in the United States, a minimum of fifteen points must have been awarded by at least three different judges with at least two three-point wins (majors) under two different judges. Depending on the number of dogs or bitches actually in competition and the geographical location of the show, a dog may be awarded from one to five points. Only one animal of each sex can win points and is designated Winners Dog or Winners Bitch. Four- and five-point majors are awarded almost exclusively at Specialty shows, which are discussed below.

POINT RATINGS

The AKC determines the number of points a win will carry in each sex and in each breed in eight different competition zones in the United States and possessions, and it will make any necessary adjustments annually. If your Bulldog takes Winners in competition, it is a very easy matter to calculate the points. Simply consult the catalog of that show and it will display the current point rating in the breed section. Make sure to subtract any absentees from the total. Dependent on the number of majors awarded to any breed in an AKC division of the country in the previous rating period, the AKC adjusts the number of dogs required so that in each division approximately the same number of majors can be awarded in a given time period.

A dog or bitch can also win points by defeating any champions present for Best of Breed or Best of Opposite Sex and those champions will be calculated to the total number of dogs defeated in the classes. If a dog that is not a champion also wins first in the Non-Sporting Group it is credited with the highest point rating for any breed in the Group if greater than its own breed total. If the dog should go on to Best in Show, it receives the highest point rating for any breed in the show.

SPECIALTY SHOWS

A Specialty show is held for only one breed and mounted by a club (either local or national) that serves the interests of that breed. Winning a Specialty show is enormously prestigious for both the owner and the

Ch. Kozabull Satuit Apple Betty, owned by Edward and Jean Kozatek and bred by Betty Davey and Jacqueline Sang.—Dave Ashbey

breeder of the dog. If the owner and breeder happens to be one and the same, then the joy this brings about knows no bounds. At Bulldog Specialties, usually only breeder-judges officiate, and, as this is a "special" event, the trophies are usually of higher quality and value than those offered at all-breed shows. This accounts for the enormous number of entries compared to those seen at all breed shows. The assumption is that the Bulldog breeder-judge will be better able to evaluate the dogs than an individual with no personal involvement and experience with the breed. In most cases, this proves to be the case.

SWEEPSTAKES

At most Specialty shows, an additional event, Sweepstakes, is scheduled prior to the regular class competition. No championship points are

Ch. Tsar's Call Me The Fat Man, owned and bred by Jim and Zoya Cardello, was the sire of seven champions, including Ch. Tsar's Fat Man's Finale, Best of Breed at the 1991 BCA National Specialty.—Chuck Tatham

awarded, but prize money is distributed along with ribbons and trophies. Sweepstakes are usually judged by an experienced breeder, who, by accepting the invitation of the show-giving club to judge, is indicating a possible intention to seek AKC judging approval at some future time. The Sweepstakes competition is limited only to young dogs and bitches, with the maximum age set at eighteen months. The classes for both sexes are six to nine, nine to twelve and twelve to eighteen months. A winner is chosen from each class, so that six dogs are in the final competition for

Ch. Kan-Do-Katie of Killarney, owned and bred by Clyde and Betty Anderson. —Jayne Langdon

Best in Sweepstakes and Best of Opposite Sex to Best in Sweepstakes. Although championship points are not awarded, Sweepstakes competition is very popular, particularly among breeders, who study all the dogs carefully and compare young stock of others to their own. Sweepstakes finalists usually draw considerable attention as contenders to be future headliners in the breed.

REGULAR CLASSSES

Seven separate classes are offered in the regular competition at shows where championship points are awarded. It should be noted that at some shows the puppy classes are combined, giving only six classes. These classes apply to both dogs and bitches and are judged in the following order:

Puppy, 6 to 9 months

Puppy, 9 to 12 months

12 to 18 months

Novice

Bred by Exhibitor

American Bred

Open

Following the Open class the Winners class, referred to earlier, is judged. In this class, the winner of each of the above classes comes back into the ring to compete against the others for the point(s). The winner of this class is awarded the point(s) and receives a purple ribbon. The judge marks his or her judges' book with the winner's armband number, and the winner exits the ring. All the other dogs in this class remain, joined by the dog that placed second in its original class to the winner of the points. These dogs now compete for the Reserve Winners placement and ribbon. This is an AKC requirement to safeguard the integrity of the awards in the event that it is later discovered that the winner had to be excused or disqualified for some infraction of the rules. Usually such infractions occur when the owner fills out the entry form incorrectly—the dog may have been entered in the wrong class, the registered number or the birthdate may not be correct, etc. In such cases the Reserve Winner is awarded the points, as, in the judge's opinion, he or she was the next best dog or bitch on that day. The result is that the integrity of the awards are not compromised.

BEST OF BREED COMPETITION

The culmination of judging is the Best of Breed competition, in which only champions of record may be entered. The Winners Dog and Winners Bitch also compete in this class against each other and the champions. From all of the assembled dogs and bitches, the judge picks the Best of Breed, the Best of Winners, and the Best of Opposite Sex to Best of Breed. It is entirely possible that either the Winners Dog or Winners Bitch can be awarded one of the top spots. As mentioned earlier, by virtue of having defeated additional dogs or bitches in the Best of Breed class, a dog may pick up additional points. At an independent Specialty show, with the exception of some special classes, this ends the competition for the day. At an all-breed show the Best of Breed winner goes on to Variety Group competition against the other Best of Breed winners in its Group. The AKC has established seven such Groups, (Sporting, Hound, Working, Terrier, Toy, Non-Sporting, Herding) based on the breeds' original functions. The Bullldog is classified into the Non-Sporting Group and often does very well against the tough competition from the Poodles, Chow Chows, Bichon Frises, Dalmatians and several others. At the end of a long day, the final seven compete for Best in Show, with one dog or bitch coming away with the highest of honors.

THE ESSENTIAL ART OF HANDLING

Anyone can show a dog, but, as in all competitive sports, some contestants are more accomplished than others. There are a few handlers, amateur and professional, who have the innate ability to make a dog or bitch "look like a million dollars" without appearing to do anything different than the routines of anyone else in the showring. When these gifted handlers are at the other end of the lead, the dog or bitch seems to exude supreme self-confidence. Daring the judge with their eyes and attitude to look at another exhibit, they float around the showring, attentive to the handler, aware of the audience, but seemingly disdainful of any of their rivals. Granted, some dogs take naturally to the spotlight, but a good handler who has worked (and played) with a dog can do wonders for its attitude and confidence.

Many dogs seem to draw the attention of the ringside before, while and after being shown. If such a dog did not win its class, or at least place higher, it is often difficult to understand why. On a loose lead, relaxed and free from any stress or anxiety provided by a nervous owner-handler, the dog or bitch is standing comfortably, appears to be well balanced and looks like an easy winner. The blame can be placed directly on the handler, who has taken an excellent specimen into the ring and transferred his or her own tension into the mind of the dog. A nervous handler will make a dog show in a similarly nervous fashion. A nervous handler who has not worked and established a personal relationship with the dog he or she will present often overshows the dog by spreading its front legs too wide, so that the dog appears out of balance. This type of handler may

Ch. Newcomb's Desert Victory, owned by Bob and Brenda Newcomb, was No. 1 Bulldog on the Pedigree rating system for 1993.

also string the dog's head up by holding the lead too high when moving and too firmly in a stacked position, especially when the judge is looking. Such poor handling will effectively give the impression of a bad topline even if the topline is excellent. The dog will usually hold this position for a short time, then, when the judge has passed by, and the

Ch. Skookum's JB Rare Annie Blair, owned by Wally and Birdie Newbill and bred by John and Susan McGibbon.—Jim Callea

handler has relaxed, the dog will adjust his or her stance in order to get comfortable, regaining the balanced, winning appearance that was displayed outside of the ring where the judge didn't get to see it.

The handler must have a good measure of self-confidence, as well as confidence in the quality of the dog being shown. These assets can only be gained by practice, not just before an upcoming show, but on an ongoing basis. Look at the drawings of the correct topline shown elsewhere in this book. Note the arch of the neck and the position of the chin— not held so high so that the layback is almost parallel to the back. Practice in front of a mirror or window in a relaxed, calm manner and allow the dog to find the most natural, comfortable placement for his feet. Do not support the weight of the head with your hand, as this will also cause him to be off balance. Instead, let the lead, with the slightest of tension, cause him to stand in place, comfortable, relaxed and self-assured. Don't fuss, allow him to look his best and enjoy your pleasure in his appearance. A well-trained show dog that the judge calls forward for examination should be looking his "stacked" best a few seconds after moving to the spot that the judge has indicated. The handler will be able to calmly listen to the judges' instructions, while allowing the judge to examine the dog unimpeded.

Ch. Chelsea's Sugar Shadow, owned by Bob and Edie Gaetner.

Owning a good Bulldog is obviously mandatory if you are to successfully show him or her to AKC championship status. However, the handler also plays a major part in the dog's campaign. Every owner or agent of a dog entered at a show has paid the same entry fee, and is entitled to equal treatment, but an accomplished, confident handler can, and sometimes does, bring in wins with average dogs over superior specimens. This occurs due to a number of factors, some psychological, some mechanical. An experienced, well-known handler, by his or her demeanor and reputation, is in an ideal position to intimidate the novice handler into nervously overhandling, causing them to pay more attention to the "expert" than to their own dog. Also, an experienced handler who knows the breed well can instantly size up the weakness in the conformation of a better dog in the ring. If this handler's exhibit is superior in this feature, he can subtly make the comparison apparent to the judge and sometimes it can help his cause.

Much is said about "dirty handling tricks" in the showring, and the practices range from excessive to barely discernible. Some handlers ask the ring steward if they can enter the ring first, stating as an excuse that their dog gets upset if another is standing in front of it. This is not the ring steward's decision, and most judges want to see the dogs arranged

Ch. Barnone's White Socks, owned by John M. Gallagher, Jr.

in catalog order before starting to evaluate each class. Amazingly, after examination and sandwiched between other dogs as the line moves back to the starting formation, the dog that started at the front appears to be quite calm and showing well. The handler of the nervous dog achieved the objective of being at the front of the line when the judge is making his or her final choice, incorrectly assuming that this gives "an edge."

Others place their dogs out of line with the balance of the class, setting their dog up a foot or two in front, which also tends to block those that are behind them. The out-of-line dog is now able to stand out as compared to its rivals. One way to combat this is for the entire class to follow suit by simultaneously moving their dogs in line with the offender, thereby drawing the judges' attention to the poor sport.

Several years ago, a well-known exhibitor was notorious for giving her dog treats, rustling candy wrappers in her free hand while in the ring. The more experienced handlers would simply place themselves between the "wrapper rustler" and their dogs, totally ignoring the practice, while

Ch. Hug-O-Bull's The Queen's Lady, owned and bred by Frank, Norma and Elizabeth Hugo, was Best of Breed from the Bred-by-Exhibitor class at the Westminster KC show in 1982 under judge Alfred E. Treen.—John L. Ashbey

the more innocent handlers allowed their dogs to watch the performance with more than a little interest. Not surprisingly, when the judge went down the line for a last look before cutting (reducing) the class, the sound of candy wrappers could be heard, so that a few of the dogs were paying little if any attention to their handlers, and left the ring ribbonless.

During BCA National Specialty events, another veteran handler employed a clever stratagem in the huge, time-consuming Best of Breed classes. This handler was known to show an occasional dog that had to be carefully watched, due to what was termed an "inconsistent" temperament. Invariably, the dog would "act up" at some point early on in the proceedings, so that all present were reminded to be wary of the dog. Later on, if the dog made the cut when the class was reduced in size and huddled together in a corner of the ring while the other sex was being judged, the handler would clip on an extra length of lead. This gambit allowed the

Ch. Bowag's Po'lar, owned by Beverly and O'Neill Wagner and Nancy Schultz and bred by the Wagners and William Hinkes, is shown at the start of a truly memorable show career. Here she was owner-handled to Best of Breed from the six to nine months Puppy class at the Bulldog Club of Philadelphia Specialty in 1985 under judge Birdie Newbill. The trophy presenter was the late "Hinkie" Bredt.—Dave Ashbey

dog to wander unrestricted in a larger circle, creating havoc among the other dogs, many of which had difficulty in settling down again for final judging. Sincere apologies were offered, of course.

When showing under canopies, in tents, or in small indoor rings, overcrowding often occurs. The dogs and handlers get bunched together, and as a result the more timid (or considerate) handlers are less likely to be able to present their dogs to their best advantage because their dogs are blocked out either by other handlers getting in front of their dogs, or by open jackets that cascade over the next dog's body. It is not unusual for a dog to have a competing handler's buttocks obscuring his face. Politely asking the handler in front to leave some room often goes unheard, due to the "concentration" of the offending handler. A considerate judge will insist on all handlers leaving enough room between themselves and any adjacent dogs. If, however, the judge fails to do this, the best recourse is to quietly move your dog to the end of the line and set him up again. By so doing, an advantage may be gained, as you can choose a better angle to show off his good points.

On temperament, the Standard says that the Bulldog's demeanor should be "pacific and dignified. These attributes should be countenanced by the expression and *behavior*," and the Standard means what it says. The Bulldog in the showring, when relaxed and awaiting examination by the judge, can lie down, roll on its back, sit down or do whatever is appropriate without disturbing the other dogs. It is not undignified if a dog is lying on his back receiving a belly rub. However, handler-encouraged barking and tug-of-war exhibitions with the lead, calculated to distract the judge and the dog that is being examined, along with other such antics, are not amusing. These antics could be construed as a form of double handling, and should not be tolerated. Unfortunately, some nonbreeder-judges who are accustomed to judging the dignified Bulldog and do not know the Standard well are taken in by these "cute" practices, to the detriment of the good sports and the breed. Bulldogs are not cute, they are dignified.

BECOMING A DOG SHOW JUDGE

For anyone who wishes to become an approved dog show judge, the American Kennel Club's minimum requirements to apply for a first breed is referred to as the *10-4-2 rule*. A prospective applicant must be able to document ten years of serious activity in the breed, proof of having bred four litters of the breed and having bred two champions of the breed. Other requirements include having judged a number of AKC-sanctioned matches and/or sweepstakes for the breed, and served as a ring steward at several shows where championship points were awarded.

If one feels sufficiently qualified, and has the desire to judge dogs, all one has to do is write to the American Kennel Club requesting an application. The application requires proof of the qualifications given above, complete with registration and litter numbers, and the names and dates of the shows judged or stewarded. The applicant also has to provide the names of two qualified breed judges who can attest to the applicant's expertise in the breed. An open-book test has to be completed from *Rules* and Regulations Applying to Registration and Dog Shows and other reading materials that AKC will provide. At first glance the test appears to consist of simple multiple-choice questions, but each question must be answered absolutely correctly. All forty-eight questions are derived from statements in the Rules. Many questions will have subtle differences so that if one has not studied the Rules thoroughly, it is easy to make a mistake. Only four incorrect answers are permitted or the applicant must reapply to take the test six months later. Having passed the test on the Rules, the AKC has the applicant meet with a member of the executive field staff for further examination, including oral and written tests on the breed. All being well, the applicant's name is published on the Secretary's Page of the AKC Gazette as having been accepted to judge the specified breed on a provisional basis.

Interested parties are given a specific time period in which to write letters to the AKC regarding their opinion of the applicant's fitness or lack thereof to judge the breed. Upon the request of the applicant, the letters will be forwarded to him or her by the AKC. The next step is that the applicant's name is published again in the Gazette with an assigned provisional judge's number. A provisional judge must complete five assignments before making application to be granted regular judging status, then must wait another year to make application to judge any additional breeds he or she may be interested in.

An AKC-approved judge may not solicit judging assignments, but must wait to be invited to judge by a show-giving club. This may take some time, as most judging panels are assembled a year or more before the date of the show. All judges are bound to conduct themselves according to the Guidelines for Conformation Dog Show Judges, and must project an unwavering air of integrity and ethical behavior that protects the reputation of AKC dog shows as fair and well judged. Judges are advised that their personal conduct, relative to potential exhibitors prior to judging, can be misconstrued by others. Therefore discretion must be exercised in all situations where judges and exhibitors are likely to come together.

A JUDGE'S RING PROCEDURE

The judge will usually inspect the ring to decide how to examine and gait the dogs, before going over the first class. At outdoor shows there are often

Ch. Skookum's Precious Panda, owned by Wally and Birdie Newbill.—Roberts

holes or bumps in the grass that are not immediately apparent. At indoor shows there are usually mats upon which to gait and examine the dogs, such that some dogs aren't at a disadvantage as compared to others. The spectators are also considered. The judge, whenever possible, will attempt to allow the ringside a clear view of the dogs. They have paid to see a show, and their enjoyment and support is appreciated by judge and exhibitors alike. Each judge will not necessarily utilize the ring in the same way, so it is beneficial to the handler to observe the judge's ring procedure before showing under the breed judge of the day. By so doing, the handler will know in advance where the judge wants the dogs set up for examination, and whether or not to go up and back, make an "L" or form a triangle. Forewarned is forearmed.

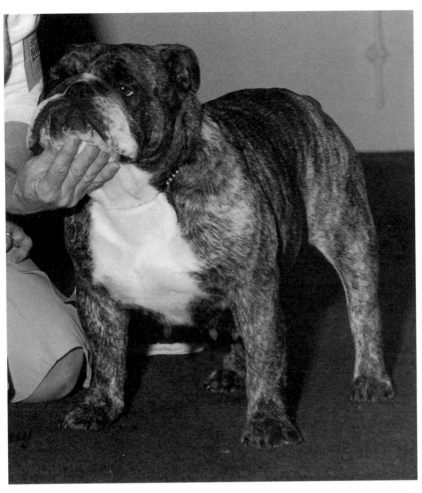

Ch. De-Gro's Winnie of Kelly Road, owned by Dean and Grovene Anderson.—Missy Yuhl

When a class enters the ring the judge will mark his book for those present as well as for any absentees. The judge will start by having all the dogs in a class gait around the ring together once or twice. This provides the judge with the opportunity to get a general impression and to look for any obvious lameness. The dogs may have traveled in crates some considerable distance to get to the show, so the opening gaiting gives the dogs a chance to loosen up and stretch their muscles if they haven't already done so. To the experienced eye, one or two dogs may immediately stand out from the others, both to the judge and the knowledgeable ringside observers. At the start of a class, the judge's heart may skip a beat upon seeing a dog that appears to be correctly balanced and is moving impressively. However, he or she must disregard this momentary impression, and upon examination give each exhibit the same time and consideration.

A Bulldog with a large impressive head on a body that does not support the head in terms of overall balance must not be given precedence over others, even if the dog is obviously young with the probability that upon maturity the dog will achieve the beauty that is basic to a well-balanced specimen. The judge is going over the dogs and evaluating them as they are on that day, and is not rewarding the potential of any given exhibit. Surveys of experienced, respected breeder-judges all show the same results; the most expert judges look for and reward the balanced dog in their rings. The Bulldog Standard states that "the points should be well distributed and bear good relation one to the other, no feature being in such prominence from either excess or lack of quality that the animal appears deformed or ill-proportioned."

Interestingly, nonbreeder-judges seem to have a much higher tolerance for Bulldogs that limp in the showring than do breeder-judges. Todays' Bulldog is a much healthier, sounder animal than was the case twenty or thirty years ago. Again, this is probably due to the ready accessibility of the best, soundest stud dogs for breeding to the best, soundest bitches, and the educational efforts of Bulldog clubs, particularly that of the Bulldog Club of America's Education Committee. A few all-breed and multibreed judges, not intimately familiar with the breed, seem still to cling to the opinion that Bulldogs are man-made crippled creatures anyway, so they ignore limping dogs, provided they meet other criteria that fits these judges' agendas.

A DISCUSSION OF IMPORTANT JUDGING CONSIDERATIONS

High tail sets can greatly affect the rear movement of the Bulldog, giving the dog a stilted, tiptoed gait. The Bulldog's tail should be rooted, when viewing the dog from the side, well below the dip behind the shoulders, and placed in such a manner as to appear to "fall off" the dog. The tail is an extension of the spine—it used to be referred to as the rudder—and should completely cover the anus. If this spine extension is so high as to be placed at the sacrum, then the pelvis will tilt forward and out of proper alignment and the legs will tend to go out well behind the imaginary line running perpendicular from the rump to the ground. This dog's stifles are too straight, so the gait is stilted, which is most improper. The dog cannot get his feet under him, so he tiptoes when he moves. The writers of one hundred years ago referred to the screw tail as "an abomination." It may be that because the screw tail went unpenalized by judges over the years, we have the high tail sets now so prevalent, spoiling the profile of so many otherwise good Bulldogs.

When observing the Bulldog's front movement, each foot should touch the ground with the outside of the foot directly in line with the shoulder, in much the same placement as when the dog is standing at ease, but not in the stacked position. The dog has to grip the ground with his paw in order to propel forward. Therefore, if a Bulldog gaited with his feet too far apart he would bounce from side to side without bringing his shoulder muscles into play. The Standard states that the Bulldog's style and carriage are peculiar, but not to the degree just mentioned. The loose-jointed, shuffling, "sidewise" motion gives the characteristic roll that is caused by the wide-set, shorter front legs being followed by the narrow-set, longer rear legs making the skin roll from side to side of the gaiting dog. The hips are much narrower than the shoulders, forming the pear shape, causing the hips to move from side to side as the dog is gaiting away from the judge. If the Bulldog does not possess the short, relatively straight, heavily muscled forelegs, then the front feet tend to come closer together when gaiting, sometimes referred to as "knitting." This too is incorrect movement and is most unattractive. Another contributor to this type of faulty movement is shoulder placement that is "under" as opposed to the "tacked on" shoulder, which is correct.

The Bulldog is unquestionably a "head" breed. The Bulldog head accounts for 39 out of 100 points in the Standard, and is the most distinctive head of any breed of purebred dog. The correct Bulldog head is the least understood portion of the overall dog, even by many breeders and judges. The highest number of points in the Standard is awarded to the nose, but large, wide, black nostrils on an otherwise mediocre head is just an example of a perfect nose. The nose is extremely important, bearing in mind the original purpose of the Bulldog. He had to hang onto the bull's nose, often for extended periods of time, and without the huge nostrils, he could not breathe well enough to perform his appointed function. If the skull and jaws are improperly formed, then the head lacks the correct foundation to enable the Bulldog to perform his once admired, now reviled function.

The head is understandably the most written about feature of the Bulldog. There have been dozens of futile attempts to describe the "brick head," usually trying to somehow fit a standard building brick into the unique shape that is the correct Bulldog head, being totally unaware that the brick mentioned in the old English literature was in fact a paving brick or cobblestone. Further, the brick in question was meant to be viewed out of the ground, and should be looked at face-on to get the general shape of the correct Bulldog head frontally, and from the side to understand what is meant by correct lay-back. When a judge is standing in front of a Bulldog and takes hold of the head, the head can often appear to be correct, and of sufficient mass when viewed face-on. However, all too often the judge cannot recognize that the lay-back stops just above the eye cavity, curving away toward the ears, instead of continuing straight up to the point where the ears *should* be attached to the head. It would behoove the judge to hold the head in his or her hands, and move to the side of the dog or bitch to ascertain whether or not an imaginary ruler could be placed from the lower jaw, touch the tip of the nose and continue up the *long, flat* forehead, well past the eye cavity, so that (depending on the size of the dog) the ruler is still in contact with the "lay-back" two or three inches past the eye cavity.

Those who enjoy the privilege of judging the Bulldog also bear an enormous responsibilty to the breed as the shapers and guardians of its future generations. The judge awards points toward a dog's championship, and from this, new fanciers to the breed assume that the winning dog is a representative specimen of the breed. From this also the novice fancier may decide to breed to a dog that has earned approval in a judge's eye. Judges are directly responsible for the popularity of any given stud dog in any given locality. Judges should not be aware of friends or acquaintances when officiating at a show. Too often we see important wins awarded to dogs that never take another point under another breeder-judge, to the great detriment of the breed, and the loss of faith of the new fanciers who might have become forces in the breed if they did not walk away in disgust. All too often, "loose talk" at ringside by experienced exhibitors can also cause new fanciers to refrain from attending additional shows because they assume that, based on overheard conversations, the end result of the judging was foretold by all present, so why did they show in the first place? If we love the Bulldog breed, then we must also respect all the reasons that brought us to it. The proper Bulldog should always reflect a character that is both pacific and dignified—so should those who compose its fancy.

CHAPTER

11

The Future of the Bulldog

IN THE PAST TWENTY TO THIRTY YEARS CHANGES HAVE TAKEN PLACE IN THE regulation of all purebred dogs' immune systems. The well-being of a dog basically comes from a combination of certain hormones that are based in the adrenal cortex, pituitary and thyroid glands.

In every purebred dog breed, a number of undesirable conditions are routinely encountered that may have been formerly unknown in that particular breed. These problems can range from skin allergies to major structural defects that affect the comfort and quality of life of an affected dog. An elapsed period of thirty years can amount to fifteen or twenty generations in the normal life-cycle of a dog, particularly when the reproductive activity of the animals involved is entirely up to their owners. If an owner's sole purpose is to produce puppies as a source of income without regard to preserving breed quality, the door is then wide open to perpetuating a host of inherited physical ills. These problems become chronic in a breed due to a number of factors, including ill-considered breeding practices. Using very tight inbreeding without regard to the genetic and health histories of the dog and bitch being bred is one example. Breeding two dogs with the full knowledge that either one or both

JB Rare Duchess Delilah (above) and Delilah's Vaca del Mar relaxing at Lake Tahoe.

Australian Ch. Elroston Mr. Sandman, owned and bred by Norman, Meryl and Howard Randell, was many times a Group and Best in Show winner in Australia. His ability as a sire is equally impressive, with champion offspring in his native land and in a number of foreign countries.

have, or are genetically capable of producing, medical anomalies is an unconscionable act to the serious breeder. Some breeders, in an attempt to reproduce a certain color, structure or function, can actually limit the gene pool dangerously. In their desire to fix desired attributes, they may create numerous imbalances in the gene pool itself. The most successful breeders also follow a plan of inbreeding but they breed intelligently, totally aware of the attributes and faults in their line, so that the dogs they produce are a true credit to the breed. These people do not breed for the monetary gain, but for their profound love of the breed and their own pride and self-satisfaction their work brings them. They are honestly trying to leave the breed (to quote long-time Bulldogger Delmar Shackelford) better than they found it.

Enormous strides have been made in veterinary medicine over the past decade that presage a bright future for the Bulldog. For example, it is now possible to predict by means of a simple blood test, known as an *endocrine immune blood panel*, whether or not a planned mating will

Australian Ch. Elroston Miss Hanky Panky, owned and bred by Norman, Meryl and Howard Randell, is also a Best in Show winner with an outstanding producing record.

produce "cherry eyes" or other such undesirable anomalies. One takes each dog or bitch to the veterinarian for the simple test, waits a few days for the results, and hopefully makes an honest decision as to whether or not to proceed with this breeding, based on the findings. One must realize that although the mating may produce a champion or two, it may well be time to skip the planned mating in favor of using another stud dog (possibly not your own) that has been certified free of the defect. A simple calculation can be made as to the probability of the offspring showing the anomaly and becoming carriers of the offending gene. In two or three generations it is now possible to eliminate many of the common problems now found in any breed of purebred dog.

DNA testing is now very much a factor in contemporary dog breeding and will doubtless be responsible for the future well-being of many

Ch. Juggernaut Jubilee, owned and handled by Dr. John Little, is shown being awarded Winners for five points at the 1993 Bulldog Club of Greater St. Louis Specialty under the author, John F. McGibbon.—Tom DiGiacomo

breeds if utilized in an appropriate fashion. As an example, the Department of Human Genetics at Michigan State University, which ran a study supported by the AKC, recently announced that the Canine Molecular Genetics Project had identified a DNA marker that is linked to the gene responsible for copper toxicosis in Bedlington Terriers. This disease is fatal

Raylynn's Igor's Meggie, owned by Igor and Olga (handling) Sapozhnikov and bred by Ray Duckmanton, taking a five-point major at age nine months at the International KC of Chicago under judge Jane Forsyth.—Booth/Lennan

for about 25 percent of the Bedlington breed. An additional 50 percent of the breed are carriers of copper toxicosis. About six hundred DNA markers were identified although the project was only contracted to find about four hundred markers. As the Bedlington Terrier's gene pool is fairly small, necessitating more inbreeding than in many other breeds, less variations were found between the chromosomes. The end result is that by judicious use of the DNA information, the gene responsible for copper toxicosis in the Bedlington Terrier can be eliminated in two or three generations. What wonderful news this is for the Bedlington Terrier fancy and, by extension, for all dog fanciers. Can't you see future generations of Bulldogs blessed with correct jaws and tails, normal eyes, tracheas and other external parts of the body and internal organs that are now potential trouble spots.

My editor and his wife are well-known breeders of West Highland White Terriers and recently ventured into the brave new world of state-of-the-art, scientific dog breeding. They bred their top-winning bitch to her grandsire, the top Westie sire in history. The "old man" was very aged at the time the bitch was to be bred, and a natural mating was not possible. Fortunately, semen had been collected from the stud during his prime and when the bitch next came in season, the seven-year-old semen was surgically implanted. The two daughters that resulted from this mating are reported to be thriving at this writing. Pioneering dog people such as these make it possible for others to reap the rewards of their dedication to the sport of purebred dogs, breeding the best to the best, improving and protecting the breed, so that breeders that come later have a strong genetic foundation upon which to build.

One can't help but wonder about the size and weight of future Bulldogs as compared to the current Standard. In all probability, twenty years from now many of the genetic problems will have been eliminated, and, hopefully, thoughtfulness will be the hallmark of good Bulldog breeding. Since the end of World War II, people have grown taller and larger due to a far superior diet and more leisure time to rest and enjoy the fruits of their labor. Bulldogs have nothing but leisure time and certainly do not labor, except, perhaps, during their daily walks; these should not be laborious. The food available to dogs today is formulated so that a Bulldog (or any other dog) can attain his or her maximum potential. Will Bulldogs follow in the footsteps of their human counterparts and become progressively larger? If so, what is the future of the Bulldog Standard? Should we, its fancy, permit the Bulldog of tomorrow to become the huge creature against which the Philo Kuon Standard was originally written in order to protect the integrity of the breed. Do breeders of other

Ch. Elroston Snow White, owned by Kathy Jacobsen and bred in Australia by Norman, Meryl and Howard Randell.

Big Billy Mancub the Great was a promising youngster with some respectable wins to his credit when he became a victim of a carelessly forgotten open gate. He was owned by Rudy Zuniga, who is pictured with him here.—Missy Yuhl

AKC-recognized breeds think that this may happen to their breed? No one knows for certain, but it is something to think about.

The major problem in breeding good dogs will always be "kennel blindness." Intelligent, therefore successful breeders, will always look for

Ch. De-Gro's Jubilee, owned by Dean and Grovene Anderson.—Missy Yuhl

the best, soundest, most anomaly free dogs or bitches from which to breed. These breeders, for the most part, intuitively seem to take under their wing apprentices who will carry on the ethical, intelligent breeding programs they learned about as practiced by their mentors. These are the members of the fancy who consistently breed to the most suitable stud dogs, regardless of their feelings about the dog's owner. Their ongoing successes speak volumes for their wisdom. They need not say a word.

If you would grow in the Bulldog breed and the dog sport, you must stay with the times, resisting rigidity and always keeping an open mind. Read, learn and scrupulously avoid "kennel blindness." Talking to the "old-timers" is a good way to absorb a whole world of dog lore. Certainly some of these elder statesmen and women may ramble on, but they have earned the right, and there is a wealth of knowledge to be

Ch. Burly Hollows Little Britches, owned and bred by Jerry and Susie Bennett.—Sue Baines

obtained from them. Years ago the "old-timers" were in the same place as the new fanciers of today—young, confident, full of life and brimming with enthusiasm. They have stayed with the Bulldog breed for the love of it, and made a place for you, so you can in turn make your own Bulldog history.

Love and enjoy your Bulldogs, for you are the future of the Bulldog breed.

CHAPTER

12

AKC-Recognized Bulldog Clubs

NEW PUPPY OWNERS ARE OFTEN UNAWARE THAT THERE IS A WEALTH OF BULLDOG experience, knowledge and friendship to be found in the surrounding area. To this end, the following is a complete list of all existing AKC-recognized Bulldog clubs, listed alphabetically by state. The secretary of the club will gladly provide meeting dates and times, and an application to join the club if you so desire.

Arizona
Phoenix Bulldog Club
Marlene Mishler
Box 216
Mesa, AZ 85211

California
Bulldog Club of Greater San Diego
Betty Fisher
1440 Pepper Drive
El Cajon, CA 92021

Bulldog Club of Northern
California
Linda Lupieka
3240 Arbor Drive
Pleasanton, CA 94566

Mother Lode Bulldog Club of
Greater Sacramento
Jaci Wallace
12551 Plum Lane
Wilton, CA 95693

Outside an English pub, some noted Bulldog fans gather in costume for a bit of fun. At the left is Pat Davis (Ocobo) with a Miniature Bull Terrier friend; John the Jester, Pat's kennel man, takes the center spot; and Howard Randell (Elroston) as Henry VIII with Ch. Quintic Amos of Ocobo completes the group.

A real show dog does everything with class! Here, the author's JB Rare Humphrey puts his own spin on a five-point major he won by going Best of Winners at the BCA Division III Specialty under the highly respected breeder-judge Edythe Schor.

Pacific Coast Bulldog Club
Becky Vertrees
1418 Las Lomas Drive
Brea, CA 92621

Colorado
Bulldog Club of Colorado Springs
Lee Ann Tate
2660 S. Meridian
Colorado Springs, CO 80929

Bulldog Club of Denver
Lynn Sites
30 S. 14th Avenue
Brighton, CO 80601

Connecticut
Bulldog Club of Connecticut
Jane Lamarine
61 Fairfax Avenue
Meriden, CT 06451

Florida

Bulldog Club of South Florida
Cheryl Polite
19015 S.W. 89th Avenue
Miami, FL 33157

Tampa Bay Bulldog Club
Ann Wagner
811 Southern Pine Lane
Sarasota, FL 34243

Georgia

Bulldog Club of Metropolitan
Atlanta
Mary White
741 Pebble Creek Drive
Norcross, GA 30093

Hawaii

Hawaiian Bulldog Club
Jennifer Matias
94–870 Lumiauau Street #K105
Waipahu, HI 96797

Illinois

Chicago Bulldog Club
Janet Klopp
3005 Huntington Drive
Arlington Heights, IL 60004

Illiana Bulldog Club
Mary Lou Lofdahl
909 Sheila Drive
Joliet, IL 60435

Indiana

Bulldog Club of Indiana
Betty Lilge
3667 Celtic Drive
Indianapolis, IN 46236

Kentuckiana Bulldog Club
Sheila Lutgring
Route 5
Jasper, IN 47546

Iowa

Bulldog Club of Central Iowa
Linda Shelburg
1400 Mountain Place
W. Des Moines, IA 50265

Louisiana

Bulldog Club of Louisiana
Douglas Wilson
Box 24
Carencro, LA 70520

Maine

Bulldog Club of Maine
Natalie Dewar
38 Cedar Street
Augusta, ME 04330

Maryland

Capitol Bulldog Club
Gail Cook
209 Maryland Road
Stevensville, MD 21666

Massachusetts

Bulldog Club of New England
Barbara Stultz
2 Norumbega Circle
Franklin, MA 02038

Michigan

Detroit Bulldog Club
Edward Scully
15155 Reid Road
Romeo, MI 48065

Western Michigan Bulldog Club
Diane Black
7878 Buchanan
Allendale, MI 49401

Minnesota
St. Paul–Minneapolis Bulldog Club
Lee Schulz
Route 1, Box 331
Mankato, MN 56001

Missouri
Bulldog Club of Greater St. Louis
Laura Wooten
1741 Winding Glen Drive
St. Charles, MO 63303

Heart of America Bulldog Club
Shirley Aspey
Box 6302
St. Joseph, MO 64506

Nevada
Las Vegas Bulldog Club
Gloria Johnson
2810 La Mesa Drive
Henderson, NV 89014

New Jersey
Bulldog Club of New Jersey
Ann Hubbard
321 Stone Hill Road
Freehold, NJ 07728

New Mexico
Chaparral Bulldog Club
Marilyn Kerr
2205 Clayton
Farmington, NM 87402

New York
Long Island Bulldog Club
Ron Jacobson
441 Silver Street
No. Babylon, NY 11704

North Carolina
Piedmont North Carolina
Bulldog Club
Karen Kauffman
6932 Valley Lake Drive
Raleigh, NC 27612

Ohio
Buckeye Bulldog Club
Nancy Cogley
408 Lima Avenue
Findlay, OH 45840

Bulldog Club of Greater Cleveland
Margaret Materna
1098 Hametown Road
Copley, OH 44321

Cincinnati Bulldog Club
Sharon Holl
5560 Old Farm Road
Mason, OH 45040

Toledo Bulldog Club
Richard Paul
5834 SH109
Delta, OH 43515

Oklahoma
Bulldog Club of Greater Tulsa
Debra Steele
Route 4, Box 1252-C
Eufaula, OK 74432

Ch. Dottie Wiggles of Killarney, owned and bred by Clyde and Betty Anderson, was a BCA Division III Sweepstakes winner and subsequently Best of Winners at the BCA National Specialty en route to her Championship.—Missy Yuhl

Oklahoma City Bulldog Club
Dorothy Armstrong
1401 Cedar Lane
Norman, OK 73072

Oregon
Oregon State Bulldog Club
Joanne Carder
460 NE Birchwood Terrace
Hillsboro, OR 97124

South West Oregon Bulldog
Club
Linda Kilgore
1751 Etna
Klamath Falls, OR 97603

Pennsylvania
Bulldog Club of Philadelphia
Ellie Sotomayer
43 White Street
Mount Holly, NJ 08060

Ch. Carlin's Tugboat Capt-J-Muggs, bred by John and Darlene Carlin and Jonda Zeller.
—Fox & Cook

Lower Susquehanna Bulldog
Club of Pennsylvania
Susi Kline
Box 93
Quentin, PA 17083

South Carolina
Bulldog Club of Greenville
Sharon Wilson
117 Quincy Drive
Greer, SC 29651

Tennessee

Music City Bulldog Club
Nancy Boniface
6315 Clearview Drive
Murfreesboro, TN 37129

Smoky Mountains Bulldog Club
Linda Howard
1702 Merchants Drive
Knoxville, TN 37912

Texas

Austin Bulldog Club
Carolyn Adams
11911 Hornsby Street
Austin, TX 78753

Bulldog Club of Longview, Texas
Cheryl Petty
Route 2, Box 121A
Bullard, TX 75757

Bulldog Club of Texas
Kathy Moss
8630 Wilmerdean
Houston, TX 77061

Fort Worth Bulldog Club
Ellen Pierson
4656 Riverport Drive
Fort Worth, TX 76137

Lone Star Bulldog Club
Barbara McCollum
105 Avenue K
Midlothian, TX 76065

San Antonio Bulldog Club
Sherry Wilhelm
5810 Mission Bend
San Antonio, TX 78233

Texoma Bulldog Club of
Wichita Falls, Texas
Janis Meacham
4300 Edgehill
Wichita Falls, TX 76305

Virginia

Bulldog Club of Tidewater
Pat Butcher
4714 Post Oak Drive
Virginia Beach, VA 23464

West Virginia

West Virginia Bulldog Club
Barbara Fisher
79 Pine Hill Estates
Kenova, WV 25530

Washington

Bulldog Club of Greater Seattle
Neva Guilliford
459 S. Cove Drive
Camano Island, WA 98292

Wisconsin

Milwaukee Bulldog Club
Lorene Boyes
1704 Grand Avenue
Lindenhurst, IL 60046

CHAPTER

13

A Passion for Bulldog Collectibles

To close *The Bulldog: Yesterday, Today and Tomorrow*, the final chapter presents a fascinating group of photographs which illustrate examples of Bulldog collectibles. Those presented here represent the more than two hundred such decorative items that comprise the author's collection. Numerous Bulldog "aficionados" share the author's passion for collecting, and these pieces are typical of the art, in many media, that has brought joy to Bulldog fans for centuries and continues to do so to this day.

The Bulldog is undeniably one of the most documented of all dog breeds, having been mentioned in literature as long ago as the thirteenth century, and by such towering figures of the written word as William Shakespeare. In the English newspapers of the 1800s the sport of bullbaiting was reported on in much the same way as basketball, football and baseball are today. For many years the Bulldog was pitted against bulls, rats, lions, apes, bears and even Bulldog against Bulldog.

The pre-Standard Bulldog appears under various guises, in drawings and paintings going back several centuries. The progenitor of the modern Bulldog appears in etchings, engravings, paintings and figurines dated in the late eighteenth and early nineteenth centuries. The most valuable of these are in museums; a very few are in the hands of private collectors, although occasionally a small collector can get lucky, stumbling on a bonanza or dealing with a seller who may not be aware of the value of a given piece of Bulldog art.

In the late nineteenth and early twentieth centuries many celebrated animal artists, after producing a well-received painting, would later work with engravers to replicate versions of the original work that would be within the reach of a wider audience. Thanks to stone and copper lithography, many original works were reproduced in limited quantities so that collectors of average means were able to enjoy the fruits of the great artists' work. Today, lithography is done photographically, with many thousands of copies being reproduced at minimal cost.

The two Arthur Wardles (not Wardel) shown in this chapter were stone lithographed in 1903 from paintings done in 1902 and are good examples of the type of collectibles available to the small collector. The original lithographs were done in color, and in later years were photographed and appeared in quantity as black and whites. In the late 1980s, Scorsbey's Scotch bought a number of original Bulldog paintings, some of which had been lithographed. The actual paintings sold for thirty to forty thousand dollars. A good Wardle lithograph, in color, framed and signed *in pencil* by the original artist, may be worth as much as one thousand dollars. It has been estimated that there are probably twenty-five or thirty Wardle color lithographs in the hands of collectors in the United States and England. In their anxiety to add to their collections, American visitors to England have paid as much as four thousand dollars for black and white Wardles of Bulldogs. This does not, however, add to the value of the others in existence.

Figure 1. This is an oil painting by American artist Jackie Balog, dated 1985. As an original, it may eventually have a fairly high value. The value to the author is twofold. This painting was commissioned by Frank and Norma Hugo, of Marlton, New Jersey, from clandestinely obtained show photographs of the author's two favorite Bulldog champions. It was presented as a complete surprise during the 1985 BCA National weekend, to the great joy and pleasure of the recipient. The dogs are Ch. Merriveen

Figure 1.

Windy Daze, an English import (left) and Ch. Bluntlines' Cannonade Bumble.

Figure 2. This is a 1906 lithograph of a painting by J. Peckitt and touches the life and career of the late and much-revered Marjorie Barnard, of the famous Noways Kennel in England. Mrs. Barnard was, for many years, the life president of The Bulldog Club, Inc., and was regarded as an absolute authority on all things Bulldog. She based much of her Bulldog thinking on the works and drawings of J. Hay Hutchinson. Mrs. Barnard had a painting of a red and white piebald Bulldog bitch, which was commissioned by Hutchinson and regarded by him as his depiction of "the perfect Bulldog bitch."

Mrs. Barnard stated that Hutchinson also had a painting done of a white male Bulldog by the aforementioned J. Peckitt. It follows, therefore, that this lithograph is of the same painting—a fact confirmed by Mrs. Barnard. Note the sweep of jaw, the tiny ears and the correct tail, which is sadly missing today.

Figure 2.

Figure 3.

Figure 3. This is a watercolor by Ane Zoutson, dated April 1986. The painting shows a Bulldog dam and sire and (presumably) their puppy; the Smooth Fox Terrier puppy is begging for the bone. This watercolor was purchased from Harrods in London in June 1986, under the following interesting circumstances.

Figure 4.

Two California Bulldog fanciers were wandering through the drapery and mattress section of the world-famous, upscale emporium. Simultaneously, both Bulldoggers spied this painting on a distant wall and, to the astonishment of the English shoppers, began a mad hurdling race, ducking under drapery displays and jumping on and off beds and mattresses until the prize was snatched from the wall. Perhaps unfairly, the winning contestant had previous experience—at athletic competitions in the U.K., albeit many years before.

Figure 4. This 1940 print from England, somewhat water stained, parodies Hitler's book *Mein Kampf.* The word *gamp* is an English slang term for umbrella. The British Bulldog (there never was and there is not now an "English" Bulldog) became, more than ever, the symbol of strength, tenacity and courage at the outset of World War II in Europe, particularly since legendary wartime prime minister Winston Churchill bore, to many, a distinct resemblance to the Bulldog.

Figure 5. Bulldogs of the Twentieth Century, by Arthur Wardle, is a color lithograph of a 1902 painting. These are depictions of actual dogs of the day, most of which would fare quite well in the show ring today. The dogs are (*from top, left to right*): Kentish Pride, Regal Stone, Ch. Broadlee Squire, Clansman, Ch. Pressgang, Ch. Prince Albert, Floradora.

Figure 5.

Figure 6.

Figure 6. Bullbitches of the Twentieth Century, by Arthur Wardle. This is the mate to the previous lithograph, done in the same year. The bitches are (*from top, left to right*): Baroness of Teesdale, Red Raddle, Spa Victoria, Ch. Kitty Royal, Ch. Little Truefit, Ch. Heywood Duchess, Ch. Silent Duchess. I am indebted to Mr. Dale Cook of Danville, California, for enabling me to acquire these two lithographs.

Figure 7. This piece is another World War II collectible, circa 1940, depicting Winston Churchill's head on the Bulldog's body. This item was found at a swap meet in Providence, Rhode Island. It was framed and cost the lucky buyer all of fifty cents!

An interesting sidelight regarding this piece, and only discovered during the photographing, is that it is signed "To Harman Christian" by the artist, Henri Guignon.

Figure 8. This is a very early photograph—well over a hundred years old—entitled *Everybody Loves Somebody*. It was bought at an auction in conjunction with the 1982 "Bulldog of the Year" show near London, England, at a cost of 100 pounds (approximately $160.00 at that time).

Figure 7.

Figure 8.

The story behind this photograph is that it was one of a set of three, each depicting a different pose of the subject matter. All three were discovered in a drawing room of a dilapidated insane asylum in England, just prior to its demolition. The other two photographs remain in a Bulldog collection in England.

Figure 9. Fifty or sixty years ago, the Bulldog Club of America's National trophies were sand castings of the BCA logo. The medallion on the top left is from 1946 (note that the Bulldog head is facing left) and was obtained from the late Jimmy Vaughters, who asked the author to look into making medallions for the 1980 National in Los Angeles. It was discovered that there was an existing cold stamping die in Texas, which was sent to a Pasadena, California, medallion manufacturing company. The piece on the top right is the first striking from this die, untrimmed.

Figure 9.

Although the Bulldog head is facing forward, which is not the correct BCA logo, it was decided to use this die, as the cost of making a new die was deemed totally prohibitive. The medallions shown in this photograph are the first strikings from the this die. A few years later—fortunately for the Bulldog Club of America—the manager of the die manufacturing company went home to England on an extended vacation, leaving an assistant in charge of making the supply of medallions for BCA. The *genius* in charge decided that it would be easier on the coining press to "hot" strike the blanks instead of proceeding in the usual way. In so doing, the die was "heat checked," totally ruining the appearance of the finished product. As a result, the Bulldog Club of America became the recipient of a new die with the head facing the correct way. No word on what happened to the genius.

Figure 10. This brass piece is a first-place trophy from the 1939 Pacific Coast Bulldog Club Specialty show, and was a gift to the author (in 1978) from the late west coast Dog Show Superintendent, Claire Bradshaw.

The original Jack Bradshaw, Claire's husband's grandfather, was an avid Bulldog breeder, exhibitor and judge during the early 1900s. The elder Bradshaw owned the second Bulldog ever to go Best in Show at the prestigious Golden Gate Kennel Club show in San Francisco. The year was 1917. Presumably, this is one of his trophies.

Figure 10.

Figure 11.

Figure 11. This piece is truly a treasure. It was a gift from Marjorie Barnard, from her own small but exquisite collection, and came along with a couple of Bulldog books that are almost a hundred years old. As in all things Marjorie, quality always came before quantity.

This sand cast bronze medal, dated 1875, was from the first specialty show ever conducted—that of The Bulldog Club, Inc., known as "The Incorporated." It predates the founding of the Kennel Club in England by ten years.

Figure 12. This photograph demonstrates the duplication that is now quite common in Bulldog figurines. The darker of the two Bulldogs is an original cast iron penny bank, and is composed of two pieces. Both pieces are held together by a screw that allows the bank to come apart when full. The other Bulldog is a Taiwanese solid brass copy of the cast iron bank, and as such has little value.

Figure 12.

Figure 13.

Figure 13. This figurine depicts the huge "Spanish Bulldog" of over one hundred pounds that was making its way into England in the early and middle 1800s, causing the Philo Kuon Standard to be written in 1864, and published in 1865.

Marjorie Barnard had an original copy of the first published Philo Kuon Standard, which the author videotaped in her house.

Figure 14.

Figure 14. This Bulldog head is an aluminum alloy casting, fourteen inches in diameter. This particular example was obtained in 1986 from the "Bulldog Pub," adjacent to Heathrow Airport, London, during redecorating. This pub was distinguished for the huge, gold-colored Bulldog at the top of an approximately twenty-foot-high post, visible for quite a distance away. The Bulldog statue was about six feet in length, and alas, unavailable.

As there is no shortage of pubs in England, a number of these heads became available, some of which, I am sure, found their way into the hands of American collectors.

Figure 15. This is a "Lionstone Whisky" decanter, after a Norman Rockwell drawing. This porcelain decanter is from a limited edition, issued in 1974. Note the Bulldog puppy tugging at the mailman's pants leg.

Figure 16. This porcelain decanter is undated. It was probably produced in the early 1970s, at which time there seemed to be a Bulldog decanter "fad." This decanter issue is among the most familiar to be found in Bulldoggers' homes.

Figure 15.

Figure 16.

Figure 17.

Figure 18.

Figure 17. This 1971 porcelain whiskey decanter, designed by C. Hallstammar and made in California, is an example of one of the numerous "Georgia" Bulldog items available. It depicts a Bulldog in the typical pose of a determined prizefighter.

Figure 18. The Hustler, from the popular Arthur Sarnoff series of dog paintings, has been much reproduced. This 1978 decanter contains 200 ml. of Kentucky Bourbon, and cost about forty dollars in the year of manufacture.

Figure 19. The Devil Dog is named after the United States Marines, who often refer to themselves as "Devil Dogs." This 1979 tribute also contains eight-year-old, 80 proof bourbon.

Figure 19.

Figure 20.

Figure 21.

Figure 20. John Bull. This 5¹/₄-inch Royal Doulton porcelain decanter also contains bourbon whiskey. In the early 1980s a limited number of these decanters could be obtained for about one hundred dollars apiece. "John Bull" is the British equivalent of "Uncle Sam" in the United States as a national personification. The Bulldog in this instance forms the head of the staff.

Figure 21. This *Mother with Puppies* is a Japanese piece from about 1981. The top is removable so that it can serve as a dish. There is no particular significance attached to this piece, other than the exquisite hand painting, which makes the dogs' eyes look almost real.

Figures 22 and 23. This inexpensive, unmarked jelly jar in the shape of a Bulldog is distinguished only in that the dog's tongue is the spoon.

Figure 22.

Figure 23.

Figure 24.

Figure 24. Although this 1974 decanter may remind one of the University of Georgia, it is from the "McCormick" series, made in Brazil.

Figure 25.

Figure 25. This 1975 *Mack Truck* decanter was introduced to commemorate the 75th anniversary of the founding of the famous company, which uses the Bulldog as its company logo. The decanter bears the legend "Built like a Mack Truck," a phrase that's become part of the language.

Figure 26.

Figure 27.

Figure 26. Ch. Basford British Mascot was the model for a porcelain made by the famous British manufacturer Beswick. This undated piece was bought for twenty-five dollars in England in 1974. An identical piece can now be purchased for about two hundred dollars.

Figure 27. This Bulldog chess set was designed by Mary Simon, the famous English dog artist. Both the black (brindle) and white major pieces are shown, as well as a black and a white pawn.

Figure 28. A set of brass fireplace implements of a type commonly seen in Great Britain during the 1930s and 1940s. The stand and each tool in the set has Bulldogs affixed.

242

Figure 28.

Figure 29.

Figure 30.

244

Figure 29. This six-inch-long bronze figurine of the late Mrs. Barnard's Eng. Ch. Noways Man of War is offered for sale by The Bulldog Club, Inc. "The Incorporated" also offers a head study of the same dog.

Figure 30. This is one of the three originals of "Now Captain's Lad" from the early 1800s. In 1982, while visiting a small tartan shop in Edinburgh, Scotland, the author noticed a few dusty porcelain items on a top shelf at the rear of the store. This very valuable piece was retrieved from that group, amid much complaining, by the elderly saleslady, who, upon descending from the stepladder, checked the price tag.

The lady announced that there must be a mistake. She had been employed at this shop for thirty-nine years and insisted that this "silly thing" could not be worth eighty pounds (about $130). In her opinion the price was "too dear," and she proceeded to climb back up the stepladder to replace the figurine on the shelf. After some discussion, I was allowed to make the purchase, and happily left the store followed by the remarks of the saleslady, who opined that Scots who live in America lose all sense of the value of money.

The figurine was well wrapped and lovingly carried to London, where a puppy, then eight weeks old and bought three weeks earlier, had to be picked up at the late Pat Dellar's Merriveen Kennels. Upon seeing the "Bull Beating" figurine, Ms. Dellar went into another room to use the telephone, and returned shortly with the news that she had just spoken with a descendent of J. Hay Hutchinson. Apparently, the gentleman owned the other two figurines that comprised the set, and was an avid collector who was willing to offer roughly forty times what had been paid for this "dear" item two days previously. Needless to say, the generous offer was declined.

But then, that's the sense of values that marks a true collector.